THE TALES OF A TIGER

Memoirs from the Vietnam War

Michael R. Farley

"You didn' t have it so bad in Vietnam. You were in the Air Force!"

Michael R. Farley

Published in the United States of America

ISBN 979-8-89395-820-1 (SC)
ISBN 979-8-89395-818-8 (HC)
ISBN 979-8-89395-819-5 (Ebook)

Michael R. Farley Publishing
180 Channings Lake
Dr., Lawrenceville, GA 30043 USA
mrfarley@bellsouth.net

Order Information and Rights Permission:

Quantity sales. Special discounts might be available on quantity purchases by corporations, associations, and others. For details, contact the publisher at the address above.

For Book Rights Adaptation and other Rights Permission. Call us at toll-free 1-888-945-8513 or send us an email at admin@stellarliterary.com.

Authors Note and Book Dedication

This book was written over a period of several years and is accurate to the best of my knowledge. The reader may note that there are a few redundancies of information, in some of the chapters. These redundancies help tie in and enhance the documentation of each one of the narratives that they are represented in.

As a combat veteran of the Vietnam war, I dedicate this book to my fellow comrades in arms that also participated in this conflict. Each one of us was an integral thread in the fabric of that historical tapestry. For too many of us, peace of mind has presented itself as a moving target, and the journey has remained challenging. It has been said of this tapestry, that all gave some and some gave all. We will meet again.

Contents

Introduction

Near the end of the American Revolution, a British army, under command of Lord Charles Cornwallis fell back to a defensive position at Yorktown in Virginia. They became trapped and surrounded. Seeing that further resistance was futile and their position untenable, they capitulated. A "rabble" American army and their French allies had beaten the army of the world's biggest empire. So humiliated and incensed was Lord Cornwallis, that he was in "dispose" and dispatched an aide to offer the traditional "Sword of the vanquished". As a last-minute slight to the American army, the aide attempted to give the sword to a French officer. However, the aide was directed to General George Washington, who accepted it with grace. Once the formal surrender started taking place, the band of the British army played the song, "A world turned upside down".

I had joined the U.S.A.F. when I was seventeen years old. Just after my nineteenth birthday, I found myself halfway around the world, in a place that had every negative connotation of the word "foreign".

It is a little-known fact that the U.S.A.F., in Vietnam, had its own combat trained soldiers. We were, "The infantry of the Air Force". I was a Security Policeman and a machine gunner. I was assigned to the prestigious, "Tiger Flight", in the 31st SPS at Tuy Hoa AB, Vietnam (RVN). Tiger Flight was the night shift security for the air base. We were the line of defense, standing between "Charlie" and the fixed and human resources of the military installation.

Every evening, we attended "Guard mount". This was a roll call and briefing prior to going to post or patrol. Our flight chief would sometimes have us all growl like tigers, before going on duty. Our unit had multiracial makeup. Each one of us proudly wore the unit patch, depicting a growling "Tiger".

I would go on to eventually serve three tours of duty, in the Vietnam War. My observations, participation and experiences, as we prosecuted the war, would change my life forever. I did not know that when I first stepped off that plane in Vietnam; for me, it would be the beginning of "A world turned upside down".

Prologue

It has been a long time since the last shot in anger of Americas unique war has been fired. There have been other books written and the usual good and bad media spectacles made about the Vietnam War. Too much currency was spent on misconceptions that Vietnam veterans were and are "bad karma". In writing this book, I wanted to dispel this perception. I served three tours of duty in the short lived, "Republic of Vietnam". I also wanted to show the reader the unique perspective of an observing participant of that war. In many cases "off the field" adventures are articulated. I went there as a child-man and came back forever changed. The war will be presented, as I knew it as an individual participant, on a one-on-one human experience. The evolving presentation is based on true stories. Moreover, these stories are about some of us who chose to stand in harm's way out of pride, duty, honor or purposes of personal reason. I hope that the sacrifices that we collectively made were not in vain. For too many of us, the scars will never heal. Princes and pawns fight wars. Princes wield power. The pawns wield swords and shields. In this conflict, many bore arms, and all were affected in specific ways, tailor made to everyone.

For those of us that shared the experience, it will always be a benchmark in our lives. We all had the knowledge and sensed that we were part of a pronounced, historical event. America must continue to serve as a beacon of hope and a bastion of freedom to marvel at. We are a nation of immigrants, who have begotten much greatness. We must continue to set standards of excellence for the rest of the world to emulate. We must never yield to tyranny or injustice, wherever it hides or is to be found. This experience has shown us that the projection of our military prowess must be based on certain criteria: It must be in the nation's best interest, with no hidden agendas. Initially, it must have the backing of most of our citizens. The associated costs in national stature, lives and treasure must be acceptable. Finally, there must be a well-planned and programmed "exit strategy". Speaking as a veteran of that war, it is my sincere hope that America, nor any other benevolent nation of the world, ever has another "Vietnam".

History

Vietnam is a small nation located on the Southeastern coast of Asia. As part of the Asian continent, it immerged as a distinct entity during the first millennium B.C. The Chinese conquered it during the Han dynasty. The Chinese ruled "The little brother" for a thousand years. Vietnam gained its independence in 939 A.D. and expanded its boundaries southward down to the Mekong Delta and the mouth of the Mekong River.

During the 19th century it was conquered and subjugated by the French. It was coddled together with present day Cambodia (Kampuchea) and Laos. For the next century, the area would be known as "French Indochina" and a colony of France. Because of vast natural resources, geopolitical and strategic importance, in this part of the world, it required a large military presence. This mandated the vaunted forces and expertise of the legendary, French Foreign Legion.

During World War II, the Japanese usurped the much-weakened French authority. After World War II, communist guerrillas known as "Viet Minh" waged a campaign to free their country from French colonial rule. An eight-year battle of independence ensued. The culmination was The Battle of Dien Bien Phu (March 13 – May 7, 1954). Here, an astonished and greatly humiliated French army was soundly defeated.

Geneva agreements on July 21, 1954 arraigned a cease fire and withdrawal of French forces. The country was divided into a communist North (North Vietnam) and a non-communist South (South Vietnam). This devolution also created Laos and Cambodia as individual entities.

For the next twenty tumultuous years, North Vietnam would be a proxy client for the communist world, dominated by the Soviet Union. It was led by Ho Chi Minh and his brilliant tactician, General Vo Nguyen Giap. They would battle the South. In what was to become the hot burning crucible in the "Cold War". The Republic of South Vietnam (RVN) was allied by a hand full of nations in the non-communist world. Its main benefactor was The United States of America. A generation of blood and treasure would be poured into the far away, exotic land. The Vietnam War or Second Indochina War would divide America, as this national trauma penetrated each household through the medium of television, on a daily basis. It became painfully obvious that the South Vietnamese government was permeated with corruption and that the army of the Republic of Vietnam (ARVN) was generally inept and unmotivated, with respect to the North Vietnamese Army (NVA) and their communist guerilla contingent in the south, the Viet Cong (VC).

America became weary and wary of a long and open-ended war. A politically weakened American President, Richard M. Nixon announced a so-called, "Peace with honor" settlement with its adversary, North Vietnam. Representing the United States, Henry Kissinger and North Vietnams Le Duc Tho had negotiated a settlement. There would initially be a face saving, "Vietnamization" of the war. This process called for replacing American troops, unit by unit, with Vietnamese troops. This would be done until all American forces were withdrawn and our country extricated from this conflict. At that point, the Vietnam War became the longest war in America's history. Even though the South Vietnamese complained of secret lateral deals between the American and communist counterparts, the principals signed the Paris treaty on January 27, 1973. Bound by this treaty, the United States withdrew from Vietnam and ended its military involvement when the last combat troops departed as scheduled on March 29, 1973.

American President Richard M. Nixon was forced to resign from office, due to the unpopular war and specifically the "Watergate Scandal". Hamstrung by a hostile congress, President Gerald Ford was unable to fulfill secretly negotiated concessions, "reparations" to North Vietnam. This same hostile congress would later cut off all funding to South Vietnam. Losing its main benefactor and facing impossible odds, South Vietnam basically stood alone. Seeing that the South had been abandoned and severely weakened, the North seized upon the opportunity and exploited its advantage of the now "Civil War". Political turmoil and military blunders exacerbated an already bleak situation, which would lead to an inevitable debacle. However, South Vietnam continued and fought alone for two more years. The forces of the communist North moved methodically southward. South Vietnams President Nguyen Van Thieu resigned on April 20, 1975 and fled the country, purportedly with an ill-gotten fortune. Ten days later, on April 30, 1975 the acting president, General Duong Van "Big Minh" surrendered unconditionally to the communists. North Vietnamese soldiers raised the red star flag over the former presidential palace in Saigon. South Vietnam lost the war and ceased to exist. The communist North had prevailed, the country was unified, and Saigon was renamed "Ho Chi Minh City".

Today, normal relations between the United States and the Socialist Republic of Vietnam have been restored. The second language of Vietnam is now English, and it is becoming more popular every day. Realizing that they may have united their country in war, but in doing so, lost the peace, the leadership saw a need for gradual and pragmatic change. This has been a slow evolution. The old Stalinist hardliners are dying off and are being replaced by more sophisticated leadership. Vietnam has made incremental steps to insert itself back into the community of nations. Trade between our two countries, once former enemies, now flourishes. The Vietnamese know that the Chinese dragon sits at its northern doorstep and is a historical adversary. With industrious people, vast natural resources and being strategically located in the sea lanes of Asian commerce; a "democratic" Vietnam has the potential to realize greatness. The possibility of Vietnam and America once again sharing an alliance of political, economic and military bonds is inevitable.

A Warriors Prayer

Oh Lord, on bended knees, I bow before thy awesome presence. Mayest I beg of thee to hear this plea from thy humble servant? I am a soldier, one who protects and defends my people, our land and our way of life. Although I may hold the sword and the shield, thou art my fortitude. I am man. I am woman. My skin is of many colors. My language is of many tongues. My culture is diverse, both old and new. As a soldier, I loathe the thought of war. In my heart, I find it to be an abomination. I would gladly lay down my own life for my brethren, but alas, is not my enemy also a human being and one of your children? Take this cup of fear and confusion and replace it with courage from thy immaculate hand. On the morrow, I may do battle. Should the terrible need arise and I must slay mine enemy or be slain by him, I ask for thy forgiveness and thy absolution. Thou hast blessed my heart with the knowledge, that even if I should walk away from thee, thou shalt never abandon me.

If it is your will and I should fall in battle, then I beg of thee to let it be with dignity. Even with my last breath, I will praise thy name. Lay this corruptible shell beneath the ground, hallowed by the bravery of other fallen comrades. May our souls rise again incorruptible and fly to thy sweet bosom to dwell there for time eternal. Is it not true, that when a flower dies and its seeds are buried, from this, new life springs forth? I beg of thee to give me the courage and the wisdom to enlighten me and to do my sacred duty with honor. Guide me to make the right decisions and do the deeds that are expected of me. In thy holy name, I humbly ask. Amen.

Part One – Tuy Hoa AB, Republic of Vietnam

"Tiger Flight"

Citation – The Air Force Commendation Medal

CITATION TO ACCOMPANY THE AWARD OF

THE AIR FORCE COMMENDATION MEDAL

TO

MICHAEL R. FARLEY

Airman First Class Michael R. Farley distinguished himself by meritorious service as a Security Guard, 31st Security Police Squadron, from 20 November 1968 to 1 November 1969. During this period, Airman Farley performed his duties as a tower guard and machine gunner in an exemplary manner, constantly maintaining his sector secure from ground attack and informing Central Security Control of developments and observations in a timely manner. His unstinting efforts contributed immeasurably to the excellent security provided the air base. The distinctive accomplishments of Airman Farley reflect credit upon himself and the United States Air Force.

Tiger Flight

I was at nineteen, embarking on a journey that would change my life forever. I had caught a shuttle flight from Charleston AFB, SC to McGuire AFB, NJ. This is the first time that I had been out in the world by myself, knowing no one. Many young and some older faces, in different military uniforms surrounded me. There was confusion, anxiety, fear of the unknown and a mountain of paperwork. I finally got a flight assignment on a contract commercial airline. I remember rushing to get a good window seat, on the port side of the aircraft. The flight to California was, other than boring, uneventful. After a brief stopover, we were on our way to Hickam AFB, Hawaii. It was dark, when we got there. I wanted to savor my brief time on the ground, in this paradise. I knew that this would be the last American soil I would touch or see, until I completed one tour of duty, in Vietnam. It was even possible that this might be the very last time, at all. We left and the sun eventually came out and revealed the stunning beauty of the vast, Pacific Ocean. As I was looking out of the window, enjoying the view, I was approached by a couple of young soldiers. One of them told me that his friend had never seen the ocean before. He asked me if I would be kind enough to let his friend take my seat, for a while, to check out the ocean view. I let the soldier take my seat, out of courtesy, as I was led to believe that it was just for a short period. I got up, walked around for some time and then came back. I went back to my seat and asked the soldier if he had seen enough. He told me that he hadn't. So, I walked around some more and returned, once more. As I talked to this soldier, he conveyed to me that he was not going to relinquish this window seat, back to me, as I was told. I looked around and spotted a nearby army officer. I explained to him what happened, and he went back with me and told the "squatter" to move. He begrudgingly did. Since there were only a handful of USAF servicemembers aboard, I believe that they assumed one of us was an easy mark. They were wrong. The flight to Clark AB, Philippines was a very long one. Prior to landing, we all saw the specks of numerous, tiny islands. At this stop, we were allowed a nice break and most of us bought postcards. A stewardess had notified us that the postage would cost nothing, since we were headed to Vietnam. All that we had to do was write the word "Free" where the stamp would normally go. Uncle Sam would be picking up the postal tab, from this point on. This benefit was tempered by the fact that he could also provide a free coffin, on a return trip.

The next leg of our journey would be directly to Cam Ranh Bay AB, Vietnam. We landed and then taxied over to the terminal, on the PSP or perforated steel plates, which had been laid, over the sandy soil. The tires made a somewhat crunching sound, as it traversed this medium. We eventually came to a stop. Then the head stewardess told us that it had been a pleasure flying with us and hoped to see us all back, in a year. There was collective vocal agreement among the passengers. However, as I looked around at all those faces, I felt certain that some would not survive this one-year tour. The cabin door was soon opened to the mobile steps. I will never forget the initial blast of the staggering, tropical heat, while we got off that airplane. Even though I was a son of the south, nothing really prepared me for this kind of heat and humidity. Those carefree summers back home paled in comparison and were now in the past. The moment my foot touched the ground, I became a combatant in war. All of us were covered in perspiration, before we got to the terminal for our incoming briefing. We had just flown halfway around the world and over "The Pond". While we were being briefed, the was a timely, much needed and collective burst of laughter, as we were told, "You are here as guests of the Republic of Vietnam". Most would have preferred to have been left off this "guest" list. I was careful not to reveal that I had volunteered to be here, for this tour of duty.

Of course, there was more paperwork. We finally filtered into the terminal area to wait for yet another hop to our prospective duty assignments. The first thing that struck me was there were local people, all around us. They were mostly clad in black pajamas and wore non la, conical straw hats. After I had gotten my orders for Vietnam, I constantly watched the world news. A considerable part of this was about "The War". The indigenous enemy, the Viet Cong (VC) or "Charlie" as they called him, usually wore black pajamas and sometimes attacked, without warning. This phenomenon projected itself on a much bigger scale, to our so called RVN allies and us. Little did we know then that "Vietnam" would be added to history and the world psyche, as a negative connotation. In the future, any country of means that projected its military forces into a foreign theater of combat, without majority support of its citizens, along with an exit stratagem from that conflict, would experience their "Vietnam".

As I waited, I watched these locals, ever so closely. I just knew that at any moment, they would drop their pretense, chores, etc. and break out with AK-47's and mechanically proceed to "hose us down". It was unnerving One momma san got uncomfortably close to me. She was chewing on something that had apparently discolored and blackened her teeth. It is called "betel nut" and it is the pit of a spicy, Asian fruit. It is slightly addictive and is sometimes eaten along with the leaves. I found out later that this was a common practice, for the older generation of women. Besides these optics, I counted the hours and minutes until my departure flight was ready. Most of us there in transit were green replacements and it was tense. The time passed slowly, but I finally boarded a C-130 for Tuy Hoa AB, Vietnam. We landed in a gully washing, monsoon rainstorm. It was such a mess, and it lasted an entire week. When the sun eventually came out, the astonishing beauty of the turquoise water of the South China Sea, mesmerized me. The ebb and the flow of this colorful body of water was very calming.

Prior to my arrival in Vietnam, I had spent a few weeks, back at Lackland AFB, Texas, in combat readiness training. Because of the need of those of us, with this special skill set, the training was intensive, but brief. My specific expertise was with the M-60 machine gun and we were the leading edge of what would later evolve into "Security Forces" and "Special Forces" for the USAF. Few people realize that the USAF had its own infantry in the war, and I was fortunate enough to be part of this history. As a specially trained machine gunner, I was assigned to the 31st Security Police Squadron and the very prestigious "Tiger Flight". One of my other assignments was to drive the V-100 armored personnel carrier or APC. It was a wheeled vehicle, with the body made by Cadillac, the very sweet running engine was made by Rolls Royce. There were just a handful of us that drove these and transported troops, to and from our nighttime positions. Driving this at night at high speed was a real rush, that few of my peers experienced. However, during monsoon season, the big drops of rain could be almost blinding, as well as the fat, tropical, flying bugs. We were issued googles, but they usually steamed up from the humidity and were then useless.

We were housed in metal, roofed barracks or hooch's, which were surrounded with sandbags. Subsequently, these helped insulate and radiate the heat, making barracks life somewhat inhospitable and at times, almost unbearable. Sand was everywhere and in everything. However, had there not been a war going on, this place could have been a resort area, instead of a deadly venue. In a couple of weeks, after my arrival, my brother would join me. Prior to joining the military, we had shared the experiences of seventeen years together. During these early years, there were times that were traumatic. It was comforting having a known companion there, as well.

Our social life consisted of our individual barracks time and club time. Here, on our base, the U.S. government ensured a never-ending supply of cheap, alcoholic beverages and tobacco. I can only wonder about how many addictions the American government was culpable of initiating or enhancing. I learned some good lessons, soon after I arrived. I noticed that the other guys had mosquito nets or rotating fans blowing over them, when they slept. After the first few days of waking up with mosquito whelps all over me, I went out and bought a rotating fan. Another thing was that everyone pulled their socks down over their jungle boots. I got up one morning and went to put my boots on. As I slipped my foot into a sock, there was another entity in it, as well. It was a huge, tropical bug, slithering around. From that point on, I copied the seemingly strange habits of the more experienced people. I hadn't been there very long when I began hearing a popping sound, day and night, in the hooch's. However, I found out that this sound was made by guys that were stomping on huge, fat cockroaches, which were numerous. This eliminated one problem but created another. When these bugs were crushed, a white liquid squirted out and it smelled awful. If it was during the daytime, momma san could clean up the mess. Otherwise, this strong odor lingered. Finally, our momma san brought in a young chicken that happily engorged itself with our troublesome bugs. It was a great barracks pet, for a while and very efficient. Unfortunately, it got a daily feeding of beer and one day it fatally overdosed, from enthusiastic over consumption.

Life in the barracks, to say the least, was interesting. A barracks next to ours had a peculiar problem that I will allude to later. It housed the troops that lightly manned the sentry posts, during daylight hours. There was some friction and apparent envy between these "day weenies" and us. Meanwhile, we proudly wore our prestigious "Tiger Flight" patches on our uniforms. The enmity got to the point where we were ordered to remove these coveted patches off our uniforms. Most complied, but some did not. For those of us that didn't, we were singled out and threatened with Article 15's. Eventually and begrudgingly, they were all removed. However, I have kept mine and even now, after all these years have one displayed in a very nice, decorations case.

Some of the aforementioned "day weenies" began complaining about an unknown perpetrator, fondling and groping their "privates". This was while they were all sleeping at night. The cunning and stealthy scoundrel was therefore, appropriately dubbed “The Weenie Phantom”. Such was the efficacy of the “Phantom” that he was never caught. Some of us had a fairly good idea of who it most probably was. However, to have exposed the perpetrator would have diminished the legend. Furthermore, it was a timely and well needed distraction.

Because our jobs were so crucial, it was incumbent upon us to digest as much information as we could, during our nightly “Guard mounts”. There were post assignments, last-minute changes and periodic intelligence briefings, which sometimes were so far-fetched, as to be laughable. The goal was to have sentry posts manned by more than one individual. However, a tour of duty in Vietnam was usually one year and we had people constantly coming and leaving. The training of the intricate details of our work was a hardship, considering the fluidity of manpower. Given the learning curve and the constant loss of experience through turnover, in retrospect, these tours should have been eighteen months or two years. Our flight chief constantly harped on following the nightly duty roster, to cut down on confusion and to have some semblance of order. I happened to notice one day that my name had been left off of the long roster. I didn’t quite know what to make of this, as it must have been done for a reason. So, with no work assignment and following orders, I did not report to work for a couple of days. I was in my barracks and a sergeant came and took me into the command post to have a chat with the flight chief. I was confronted about not coming in for a couple of nights. He asked me what I had to say about this. Making sure that I was covered, I produced copies of the duty rosters for the days that I missed work. I also reminded him of his constant repeating of roster vigilance and to show me my name. He looked over these duty rosters and checked it up and down for several minutes. Of course, my name did not appear, as apparently, this had been an oversight. He then angrily asked his staff what the worst sentry post we had was. One of them said “the pit”. I went to the nearby armory and picked up a weapon and ammunition etc., and a mobile patrol picked me up and took me out to this post. After I left, I am sure that the staff got an earful, as someone had unintentionally gotten over on “the man”.

We arrived at “the pit” and I was given a box of cold C-rations and knew that they probably would not be back to check on me. As my eyes adjusted to the darkness, I saw that there was sand everywhere. In the middle of all this sand was “the pit”. It was a manmade, freshwater pool, which was used to train swimmers and water rescue, during the day. Many of the sentry’s didn’t like the darkness, desolation and the fact that there was no cover, when it rained. However, someone had to be there, just in case Charlie improbably decided to access base resources, through this point. So here I was in the boondocks, guarding sand, with a swimming hole in the middle of it. The minutes that went by were like hours and the hours like days. Then, I had an epiphany. The hot sun had heated this water all day and the surrounding sand was a natural insulator. Why not throw caution to the wind and just go "skinny dipping"? So, I removed my uniform and under clothing and folded it up neatly, on the ground. My M-16 and ammo belt were placed on top of these clothes. Lastly, I turned up the volume on my two-way radio and placed it upright, next to my gear. Now, naked as a jay bird, I stepped into the water, and it was indeed perfectly warm. For the first time since childhood, I was "skinny dipping". I was now figuratively and literally in hot water, and it was glorious! Even if Charlie did happen to come through here, he would probably die of laughter, as I would have been seen as one of those strange Americans.

I am not sure how long I stayed in this pool, but I did not leave, until I was thoroughly satisfied. When satiated, I got out and drip dried, in the tropical heat of the night. Now, totally refreshed, I got dressed. It was a peaceful night. Dawn was breaking, when the unmistakable sound of an approaching military jeep was heard. Of all the people, it was the flight chief, who came to check out the latest bete noire. He had cooled down considerably from our earlier discussion. There was a mild scolding, which was also reciprocated with the acceptance of some, feigned culpability. Of course, I told him how lonely, desolate and harsh this post was. He seemed to be pleased, with respect to my new and positive attitude. He then asked me if I agreed that a week out here would in essence, reinforce my diligence to duty. I glumly agreed that it would. As he left, satisfied in his accumulative wisdom, we both turned away smiling. This had gone some distance beyond turning lemons into lemonade. It had turned hot water into…... "hot water". That week went by too fast! Naturally, I had to let my brother in on the deal. We had a good thing going, until he thought he saw an Asian tiger walk by, as he was doing a back stroke one night. At daybreak, the fresh tracks confirmed the sighting. Neither one of us requested that post, after that. The envelope had been pushed far enough.

During the monsoon season, you went to work wet, ate wet and sometimes slept wet. The howling wind, blew varying mixtures of sand and water into the barracks. You didn't leave the barracks, unless you absolutely had to. Our unit "Tiger Flight" lorded over the place, at night and we secured this important installation. We manned the machine gun bunkers, towers and worked walking and mobile patrols. The defined perimeter had razor edged concertina or barbed wire, land mines, claymore mines and trip flares. Outside this perimeter fence was a "free fire zone". Bilingual warnings were posted and anyone in these areas, during the hours of darkness, could initiate a lethal response. The K-9 handlers, with German Sheppard's patrolled behind us and other vital areas. Adjacent to this USAF installation was an American army base, which hosted the 173rd Airborne Division, as well as the crack, Korean "White Horse Division". These areas were occasionally hit by high explosive 122 mm rocket attacks. We could watch the orange, mushrooming fireballs, in the distance. This was a very powerful reminder that we were at war and no longer innocent children. The enemy was out there, present and was trying to kill, wound or damage us, in any degree possible. Subsequently, we both had our conflicting obligations to perform.

Bunker duty was the worst. After delivery, the heavy steel helmet and even heavier flak jacket came off. These wood framed, rectangular posts were usually ground level and were constructed mainly out of military green sandbags. Coarse sand was in abundant quantity. The roofs were constructed with thick plyboard, and this was sometimes covered with a layer of sandbags. The front opening faced the perimeter, and the sides were open for visual observations. Our M-60 machine guns were placed in front, as to face any potential, enemy threat. There was adequate room for an assistant gunner. Bunkers were spaced to give overlapping fields of fire. Inside, we had various colored slap flares. To trigger them, the top cap, with a center, protruding firing pen was removed and placed on the bottom. The flare was held in one hand and pointed skyward. It was then struck or "slapped" with the other hand on the bottom. The controlled blast projected the contents upward, to its highest point. The small silk parachute, then deployed and it lit up an area of an approximate city block, with ignited white phosphorous. We also had a small number of red and green flares, which we seldom used. Launching a red flair meant enemy contact, while the green flair signified end of contact or all clear. These sounded like a shotgun going off and it was a sudden and blunt force on your strike hand. After the experience of launching a few of these, I learned to strike them with my heavy steel helmet. It was much easier on the hand. Some of these bunkers had cased fragmentary grenades. Additionally, I brought an M-16 rifle and wore a.38 pistol as a side arm, on a web belt that also had a sheathed bayonet. I figured if someone wanted to try and take me out, they were going to have to really work for it.

This being said, we had to work in the elements and indigenous environment. One of the phenomena of monsoon season was the pelting, sideways rain and surface sand blasting. Then came the heat, humidity and infinite bugs. The intense heat and humidity promoted a condition that we called "jungle rot". This happened in the skin of the crotch area. It looked bad and smelled bad. Other than going to see a doctor, there was a do-it-yourself remedy. This was to constantly use abundant talcum or baby powder. I heard stories of the men out in "the bush" just walking around naked, until it dried up. Each episode caused constant itching. Because we were subjected to numerous mosquito bites, during the course of the night, many of us consumed malaria pills and salt tablets. The malaria pills would sometimes result in loose stool. The worst bites were always on my fingers. With the combination of heat and salt tablets, the salt in our perspiration would leave a thin layer of white residue on the leather parts of our jungle boots. This would be the heels and toe area, as the rest of the boot was canvas. Inside and on the bottom of these boots were punji pads, for protection of punji pits. These were small, concealed holes that were dug and cleverly concealed by the enemy. Inside of them were sharpened bamboo sticks, covered with animal or human feces. Stepping on one of these and being wounded was nasty, painful and dangerous. It was a cost-effective and natural weapon system. The insects crawling on our bodies, took some time to almost get used to, if ever. Our trousers were "bloused" to the tops of our boots, with a green, elastic band, to prevent things from crawling up our legs. The worst thing that crawled on me were scorpions. Although I was never stung, those that were said it was like a wasp sting. The gnats and hard-core flies always seemed to peak, during the consumption of, usually cold C-rations. Just an annoyance, they were casually swatted away.

However, there was one insect that was at the top of the list, in our related, misery index. These were the crab lice or "crabs", as we called them. Once you became an unwilling host for these infernal, little parasites, a few things happened. Because we worked at night, they weren't usually noticed, until the itching and constant scratching began. Many of us, scratched until we bled. Since they lived on our blood, it just exacerbated the problem. This is how annoying it was. Once you announced that you were infested, fellow service members were sure to give you some distance and wide berth. Because of the intense heat, most of us walked around in our underwear, off duty, in the barracks. Our close living confinement ensured that they would be spread to others. It was not a matter of if or when you got the crabs. It was a matter of how many times we would be individually infested. Their primary location was in the pubic hair, and some just shaved this area off. This helped to a certain extent. The common treatments were getting medicated soap from the dispensary or using our military issued bug spray and saturating the area with bug poison, which was not recommended. There was a joke that went around about a sure-fire way to rid yourself of these odious pests. It was to shave half of the pubic hair off and then set it on fire. When they came running out, just nail them with an ice pick! However, impractical and dangerous this proposed solution was, it nevertheless served as a bit of levity and dark humor.

Night duty became a real challenge sometimes, to just stay awake, as the physical and psychological stressors drained the energy from our youthful bodies. If we were fortunate enough to have an assistant gunner, then it usually wasn't much of a problem. However, most of the time we were by ourselves. It was not unusual for someone to have a lit cigarette between their fingers and discover that they were badly burned, after falling asleep and then suddenly waking up to the pain. If one of the lifers came by and found you asleep, the punishment might be harsh. It could mean filling up numerous sandbags, out in the incredible heat, for hours. We had conversations with some of the soldiers, as they came over to use our much nicer facilities. One of them told me a story of fellow soldiers on sentry duty that had fallen asleep. They had been watched by the enemy and when they fell asleep, their throats had been cut. Therefore, many of us developed the "Tuy Hoa Jerk", me included. We trained ourselves for this sleeping issue. When we happened to notice ourselves drifting off to sleep, a burst of reserve energy was used to "Jerk" ourselves back awake. I did not want to fill up sandbags in the hot sun or have my throat cut. This defense mechanism was so deeply imbued, that it became second nature. Subsequently, it is a habit that I brought back from the war and still have to this day. At times, it makes transitioning to sleep difficult.

These postings were usually around eight hours. However, during the lunar new year or "Tet" period, this was sometimes increased to twelve hours. We always looked forward to the breaking of dawn, as it indicated that the shift was soon concluding. Pick up was usually by a duce and a half truck, but sometimes, by an APC. All weapons and ammunition checked out had to be returned and accounted for in clean condition. We carefully cleaned the weapons from sand and dirt, prior to turning them in. Then we returned to the barracks and were free, until the next shift. It became machinelike, after a while.

There were various and memorable incidents that took place as follows:

One night, some of us were enveloped by a noxious, gaseous cloud, which originated outside the perimeter wire. I can remember my eyes burning, choking and coughing from this nauseous and mysterious gas. Our command structure frantically brainstormed for an expeditious solution. One of the on-duty doctors came up with one. We were told to remove our T-shirts, urinate on them and then put them over our heads. This was to serve the purpose of gas masks. I found this idea to be so revolting that I declined. I had a headache for the next couple of days and was never made privy to the long-term effects.

I witnessed the shooting deaths of two suspected, enemy soldiers. The first one was just after I heard a motorcycle in the "Free Fire Zone". I saw the two men clearly, the driver and passenger. A shot rang out, from a nearby tower and the motorcycle crashed. One man ran off, while the other was hit and died, at the scene. One of our mobile patrols went out and retrieved the body. Soon afterword's, I saw the jeep covered in blood. Part of our beachfront was mined. The other part had observation towers and walking dog patrols. One night, one of these towers called in and reported a sampan that had ventured in too close to our positions and was suspect. I saw the silhouette of this boat against the starlit night. The tower guard fired at it, and I saw an additional tracer round, hit the intended target and heard the splash. Upon daylight, a body was washed up, on the beach. There were ample visual warnings. Unlike the NVA (North Vietnamese Army) Charlie did not wear a uniform, as to blend in with the populace. These were potential enemies, Viet Cong soldiers that had been probing our defenses and they paid the ultimate price for it.

One night, my brother and I had positions next to each other. It was almost dawn, but still dark. He called in an individual walking close to the wire and was given permission to fire. I also saw this individual and waited for him to be dropped. However, as he had him in his gun sight, he saw that it was just a kid. He did not fire, and that kid was very lucky. None of us wanted to unnecessarily take a life and this would have worn heavy on our hearts.

I had my own chance to take some people out, one night. I was half awake when I heard a large truck. It was a duce and a half, with Vietnamese markings. It was casually moving in the Free Fire Zone and heading from right to left. There was an immediate confluence of both fear and excitement. As I tried to suppress the immediate emotions, mechanical training took over. The belt loaded M-60 machine gun was pulled tightly to my right shoulder and targeting was acquired on the moving driver. I intended to neutralize the occupants in the front cab and then whoever was in the back, as well. My finger was on the trigger and I requested permission to open fire. The radio came back to life and crackled "hold fire!" An adjacent tower put a spotlight on it and the truck came to an immediate stop. A jeep patrol quickly responded and went out and confronted them. As it turned out, those in the truck were drunk Vietnamese soldiers, on their way to a local bordello. They had foolishly taken a well-lit shortcut, through our Free Fire Zone. This could have resulted in all their deaths. Although I would have been in the right, I would have been haunted by this "friendly fire" incident for the rest of my life. Even now, there are lingering nightmares of not holding fire and killing these men.

There was one specific bunker that no one wanted to get assigned to. It was near a low-lying area that served as a garbage dump. Rats roamed over the place, and they were huge. The possible disease infested mosquitoes and crawling bugs were bad enough, but these rats made it downright creepy. Many of the positions near this area had "rat boxes". That is red rectangular boxes, that were hollow inside and laden with very potent rat poison. Whenever I got this post, I always checked out a shotgun. This was not for protection from the enemy, but from rats. I will never forget the night that I was attacked by rats. A mobile patrol had just delivered my cold C-rations. The primary contents were canned and usually consisted of the following: A main meal/meat, fruit and a small cheese can, with a soda cracker pack. There was a brown, plastic bag that had gum, salt, pepper, a small box of four stale cigarettes etc., and a plastic eating utensil that looked like a hybrid spoon and fork. We all had service issued can openers. They were small and could go on a key ring. They were sometimes referred to as "P-38keys". I was doing fine, until I opened the small can of cheese and sat it down, on the front opening of the bunker. I soon heard a rustling sound, but already knew what it was. When I shined my flashlight, I saw a huge rat; its eyes appeared to be red and almost demonic, by the light. It seemed to have no fear, as it made its way towards the opened can of cheese. These are very intelligent animals that sometimes send in an "investigator". In astonishment, I momentarily froze. Collecting myself, I slowly removed my bayonet from its sheath. This monster was just inches from me but showed no fear. I raised the bayonet up and grabbed the hilt with both hands. In a single, downward thrust, I ran it through and pinned it to a sandbag. What startled me was that it then began squealing loudly. Subsequently, I then also heard more and numerous rustlings outside. When I shined my flashlight into this area, I saw numerous, beady red eyes rushing forward. Now, under probable attack, I grabbed the radio and immediately left the position. I was able to contact a patrol and it seemed like an eternity for them to come. I told them what happened, and I finally went back. There was a dead rat, pinned to a sandbag, but its buddies were now gone. I spent the rest of the night on the roof of that bunker. When morning came, I went and retrieved my bayonet. The rat was well over a foot long, from head to tail.

In this part of the world, there were much fewer inhibitions with respect to the human body. As I alluded to earlier, in the barracks, we alleviated some of the heat misery, by casually walking around, in our underwear. Our common latrine was a separate, open building, with toilets on both sides. The associated shower room inside was also open. There was no such thing as privacy, either. It wasn't unusual to be sitting on the "throne" and have a momma san tap your feet, for you to lift them and she could sweep. Personally, the hardest thing to get used to was showering, while various momma sans came in on you and hand washed clothes. Sometimes a pair would come in and begin to giggle. After I got used to it, we all giggled.

The latrine was also a unique source of information and current events. This information could be gleaned by reading the latest words of wisdom, by authors unknown, on the walls. Of course, there were the basic, anatomically correct art; sometimes lewd and exaggerated. One morning, after hearing loud and sustained laughter, I decided to investigate. There had been a recent series of handwritten "articulations". One stated: "Flush real hard, the officers chow hall is a long way off". Another was: "Will trade two blind crabs (lice) for one that can see." However, the one that had everyone rolling was a very clever "physics formula". It was as follows: "The heat of the meat, plus the mass of the ass… is equal to the angle of the dangle!" This marvelous enlightenment had led some to immediate, tear flowing laughter. Some of the other memorable ones will not be repeated here, due to the graphic nature of the material.

We had one TV and one radio station. They were part of the military's Armed Forces Vietnam Network or simply AFVN. There are a few things that I remember about these. The TV programs had absolutely no commercials in them. However, AFVN would periodically throw in several minutes of back-to-back commercials, upon request. At the end of evening programming, both the national anthems of the Republic of Vietnam and of the USA were played. Sometimes, there was a narrated video of the poem "High Flight". It was a TV sign off and I always found it to be both patriotic and moving.

Although Vietnam was a country at war, the scenery was that of a lush, tropical and ancient land. The city of Tuy Hoa (two-e-wah) was a very old, coastal town. Most houses were constructed of block and stucco, while the roofs had barreled, terra cotta tiles. On the outside of town were third world, straw hut villages, surrounded by rich green, rice paddies. Their appearance was something that may have looked the same, for centuries.

Monsoon Tea Time

Going into the city of Tuy Hoa required a few things. We had to exchange our MPC or military payment certificates into Vietnamese currency, at the bank. Wearing the 1505, khaki dress uniform was required. We had to get a ride to the main gate and then somehow get a ride from there, into town. It required some effort and transportation was usually from a military vehicle going that way. I once got a memorable ride from two Korean captains that seemed to believe that there was no speed limit and that they owned the highway. However, that was a singular exception and not the rule. Inevitably, and by popular demand, there would usually be a USAF blue bus service. The ride into town was scenic and interesting. Going down Highway One we could see both the ancient and modern world. There were beautiful rice paddies and people with water buffalo in their black pajamas, bent over and working in them, as they had done millennia ago. This optic was a post card representation of rural life, in most of the country. Most of these small dwellings were thatched roofed. There was a river bridge that had one lane on it and traffic was intermittently alternated to adjust as needed. The "white mice" or Vietnamese civilian police regulated the flow. We were let off at the edge of town and were immediately set upon by hustling "minders". These were hard core kids who spoke broken English and would guide and assist us for expected fees, commensurate with their services rendered.

A list of goods and services that could be procured were nonchalantly rattled off, starting with all things illegal and immoral. This was not their first nor would it be their last rodeo. This kind of hustling gave them both scratch to spend and cumulative, street cred. As there were no social safety nets here, aside from the Confucian mandated large families, kids hustled to pool resources and make ends meet. Each of these families was a collective unit. As we made our way through the city, there were the sights of a very old Asian metropolis. There was also a smell of charcoal and lemon grass in the air. We encountered pedestrian pigs, ducks, geese, along with roving cats and stray dogs, with their indigenous bent and curled tails. Since the locals had been exposed to Americans before, they appeared to barely notice our intrusion into their world or show any signs of typical curiosity. However, this was subliminal and belied this apparent lack of curiosity. They knew exactly who we were, how many were in our "entourage", where we went, where we did not go, what we wanted, bought etc. The eyes and ears were numerous, yet invisible, but always there.

On this city visit, I was accompanied by a friend. After our visit and on our way out, we had to occasionally take shelter from several hard rain showers. It was monsoon season. This meant that it was cooler after the rain. The thunder and lightning of these storms could be violent, and it could rain for a few minutes or a few days. Our visit had ended; we had a good run. So, with our current needs satiated, we made our way back to our starting point. The dark clouds begat rumbling, vibrating thunder and impressive lightning. As the skies opened, the very hard driven rain soaked us thoroughly. The one or two kids still with us guided us to shelter, which was the overhang of a barrel tiled roofed dwelling. Pressed against the wall of this building, we waited. The rain did not let up. We had been there for some time, when an old man appeared at a doorway and gestured for us to come inside. He spoke no English and we were somewhat apprehensive. Were we being set up? Did this "kindly" old man just beguile two naive, American servicemen for kidnapping, torture or worse? Only one thing was apparent, once inside, we were out of the hard, driving rain and in a dry place. As my memory serves me, I believe that we were given cloths to dry off. Hot tea was brought in small, covered porcelain cups. It was served hot, but diluted, Asian style. We both thanked our timely host for his unexpected benevolence. With the authority of a house patron, he said something in Vietnamese to a young girl that I did not catch. The next thing we knew, a Sears catalog in English was presented to me. The covers and some of the pages were torn out, but enough was there for me to feign obligatory interest, while thumbing through it. He rambled on and some of it was occasionally interpreted by our minders. The hot steamy tea kept coming and was politely consumed. Finally, after some time, the rain stopped. We got up to leave, politely bowed and thanked our rescuer host profusely.

We made our way to Highway One and caught a ride back to the air base. We passed the same tropical flora and fauna, but I didn't notice. I was consumed in thought about the incredible and unforgettable gesture of kindness from an old Vietnamese man, that didn't know me. We were foreigners, outsiders, a commercial endeavor for some and outright enemies for others. Everyone locally would know what he had done, because nothing got past them. This was a teaching moment. Some things transcend culture, ethnicity and politics. A poor old man from a different world, put himself and his family at risk to be thoughtful, good hearted and brave. This took place in 1969, towards the end of my first of three tours of duty in RVN. I will not forget this unexpected kindness, extraordinary humanitarian act, and I will always remember it as the "Monsoon Tea Time".

The Korean Restaurant

The best restaurant in the city of Tuy Hoa was simply known to us as The Korean Restaurant. Its patrons were mostly Vietnamese of relative affluence, Koreans and Americans. The average locals were somewhat priced out. Here was the place where we sampled the local dishes. Because of the Korean influence, dog meat was served, sometimes. We jokingly referred to it as "Seoul Food". During one of my visits to this establishment, there was an experience worth noting. It was not unusual for us to work all night and then go into town. We could return and get a nap, before going back to duty. On this occasion, I had gone into town with a friend. We visited the usual places. After dropping by the catholic run orphanage to play with the kids, we decided to finish up by going to this Korean restaurant. Here, we often chose dishes blindly off of the menu, which was in Korean and Vietnamese. The service was always very good. Sometimes not knowing what to expect, we had to sometimes look around and observe our fellow patrons. Our order came. It was a pot containing hot charcoal and it was carefully placed on our table. A perforated metal grill was placed on top of this hot charcoal. The metal grill resembled a large funnel, turned upside down. At the base was a lip that went all the way around. As the metal was heated, our server, using chop sticks, carefully placed the strips of meat, on this small stove. As the meat touched, it made hissing sounds. This meat had been marinated with lemon grass, garlic, spices and oil. When done, the cooked meat was placed on a bed of rice and crushed peanuts were sprinkled on the top of this. Seasoning leaves and nuoc mam (nook mom), a fish sauce made from anchovy extract were at our disposal. This indigenous seasoning enhanced the experience. No Vietnamese family was without nuoc mam. The best came from the Vietnamese island of Phu Quoc. This had been one of the most, if not the most delicious meals I had ever gotten there.

I had noticed, in our visits to the restaurant, that groups of local people were burping, periodically. On the surface, it appeared that those culpable, were without benefit of good table manners. However, this was not the case, as it was a cultural expression. I learned that if a family or close friend were enjoying their meal and felt comfortable, burping let those present, feel and share this confidence of purged inhibition. In essence, their comfort zone was audibly expressed, to be shared. This "mannerism" was employed only by adults.

While this observation was happening, my stomach started to rumble and have a conversation with itself. It was during the second helping of food that it really hit me. I had to repeat the words "rest room", while the proprietor looked it up, in his well-worn, bilingual dictionary. Finally, with a nervous laugh, he pointed to the back of the building. He said something to a kid, that came forward. This kid led me to an area behind the building that was out in the open. It was adjacent to a lush, green series of rice paddies. It was close to harvest time and the individual stalks were loaded with unpolished rice. So here, out in the open was the so called "rest room" and something which I had never seen before. It consisted of a concrete square, with two sets of elevated foot pads, on an incline from toe to heel. One set of foot pads was larger than the other. I made the assumption that one was for adults and the other was for children. Immediately behind each set of foot pads was a circular hole that was an opening, into a hand dug, earthen septic tank. Coming out of each hole were hordes of winged insects and a stench that was overpowering. At first, I thought they must be joking. However, they were not and as the window closed, it was the only option. I now longed for that special purpose, G.I. "throne" and all that associated, soft paper that was still there and hadn't been ripped off by momma san yet. However, "Grizwald" would have none of this. Grizwald is the little guy that lives in your bowels. He mercilessly slashes away with a sharp implement, when nature calls abruptly. I was going to have to make a dash for it and the timing was going to be close.

Suddenly, everything became oblivious, with respect to satiating nature. If there was a God in heaven, I knew that I would be allowed to make it, despite all of my unrepented transgressions. Grizwald was all that was evil in this world and all that mattered, as his unequivocal demands had to be met. The last ten yards were made in a couple of bounds. Yes, those years on the high school track team were now paying off. What came next, will be put into, military aviation analogy.

Having a clear visual, the pilot approached and locked in on the assigned target. Despite and disregarding heavy enemy flak (flying bugs), it was a go for bomb release. Notwithstanding apparent near misses, from previous missions, this one was a done deal. Oh yes, there was a God in heaven, indeed. Now, there was blissfulness, peace and all was well in the world. Or was it? As every military aviator knows, the mission is not complete until the paperwork is done. There was an immediate problem that now had to be addressed. Here I was, confident in the belief that the "mission" had been carried out. However, there was NO PAPER in sight, to finish the job. Therefore, after deep thought, an epiphany was generated, with respect to this conundrum. Out of necessity, the "facility" of this venue was accessed and out of necessity the subsequent matter was resolved, with satisfactory expedience. Going native in this open environment was a unique experience and would never be repeated. However, with the knowledge that unseen eyes here were ubiquitous. It is entirely possible that the legend of the "Harvest Moon" may have been born and thus precipitated wagging, foreign tongues, for generations to come.

Also, the food that we had been served, by a random choice, was simply delicious. The meat was not fish, pork, chicken and for practical reasons was unlikely to be beef. Therefore, using the remedy of deductive analysis and the contemporary Korean proclivity for cooked canine, I believe with some certainty that were served and consumed dog meat. Although this restaurant was visited a few times, that item was not chosen again. This had been the highlight of the day and was nice. We caught the blue bus and returned to base. This was a memorable visit.

In addition, I would also like to mention that there were other people and places that were visited in this nice old city. There was an older lady, who ran a small shop that we referred to as "Madam Rouge". She apparently had experiences with members of the French community, during the previous Indo China conflict. It was obvious that she had acquired a taste for French cosmetics and wore rouge makeup. The application of this makeup was layered, as she sought to arrest time. Certainly, she must have been a real beauty in her youth. Subsequently, she was very amenable to young American customers, as well. These were but a few of the local characters. that we encountered

Harvest Moon

We were placed in a faraway war. And hadn't seen the likes before. Our job was tough, and our nemesis mean. Who was this foe we had not seen?

The seasoned veterans knew the ropes. Back to "The World" was in our hopes.

This tropical place was upside down. To get relief, you went into town.

We chose our food off the menu, and I'd soon be seen at another venue.

Where's "the room" I did enquire? I ran so fast; the straights were dire.

I sat down and not too soon, but the native sun, saw the "Harvest Moon".

Different Worlds

On July 20, 1969, a slim teenager was wearing an American uniform, in a foreign country, at war. I was on duty at my dark post, a machine gunned, sand bagged "hole"; with a small roof and on the perimeter of Tuy Hoa AB, Republic of Vietnam. Night duty or graveyard shift, in the civilian world, was where all the action was. Facing me, in the darkness were very unfriendly eyes, intense heat, humidity, malicious bugs and other pesky varmints. At times, a nice sea breeze, from the astonishingly beautiful, turquoise and sometimes capricious, South China Sea would bring periodic relief. The vampire, blood sucking mosquitoes would encounter a natural crosswind that would momentarily blow them off course from their intended targets. We were their U.S. government provided buffet. Our involuntary blood donations were daily and our collective sweat, moistened our uniforms and the indigenous ground.

It was a perfectly clear, moonlit night. The military chatter, on the small, issued radio was at a minimum. This was an extraordinarily momentous time in history and the eyes and ears of the entire world were watching and listening. None of us were allowed to have "Fox Mikes" or FM civilian radios. That was against strict, military regulations. This was so that all focus could be on our barbed wire and mined, perimeter and the enemy. However, my "Fox Mike" was working perfectly, along with everyone else's (snicker). Security control was giving us frequent radio updates of the Apollo moon landing. The "Eagle" had separated from the command module and had begun its descent to the surface of the moon. We all watched the bright, full moon, held our breaths and listened, with the rest of the world. Americans Neil Armstrong and Buzz Aldrin descended into the unknown and history books. With much relief, the words came, "The Eagle has landed". There was the sound of cheers, all around me, at this astounding accomplishment. The two American astronauts worked professionally and methodically. The planet then waited anxiously for the second act, which none of us will forget. "That's one small step for man, and one giant leap for mankind".

Here we were, uniformed Americans at war and halfway around the world, breathlessly listening to other Americans, on the moon. As I looked up at the bright clear, full moon, it was astonishing that someone was now walking on the surface. It was really happening now, and this was a once in a lifetime contrast. This historic event just seems like an incredible dream now. We were serving in a war-torn country and astronauts were walking on the moon. It was a dichotomy of two different worlds. I was very young then and this event left a positive and indelible mark on my memory. What comes to mind now is “Tempus Fugit”.

Australia

One of the things the military did to improve morale was to allow us to have rest and recuperation leave or simply R&R. We were allowed one week to visit various countries of our choice, around the Southeast Asia Theater. There was never any question where, but when I wanted to go. As a child, I had always wanted to go to Australia. We had been in the country approximately 10 months and were counting down the days on our "short" calendars. The calendars were given to people who were "short" i.e., close to going home. They started at one hundred until the days were counted down to zero. Sometimes one would be startled by a "short timer" yelling "short!" This could take place in the mess hall, theater, church, latrine or barracks. Those who were not short looked upon them with jealousy. Everyone knew the days they had been there and the days they had had left. New replacements were called "new bees." We had purposely waited until we were "short" to go to Australia. This would be the reward we had given ourselves for running the war gauntlet and physically surviving.

Going, would be my brother, Bill and I. Bill was a friend from Ohio. We had all started our tours about the same time. We packed the few toiletries and civilian clothes we had for the trip. There was a minimum amount of money required and it had to be shown before we left. We caught a C-130 hop to Cam Ranh Bay A.B. where we were briefed and made ready for departure. Here, were soldiers, sailors and airmen from every branch of service and every allied country. We met some Aussie officers who were some real down to earth people. They suggested places for us to go to and see.

Our "Freedom Bird" was a beautiful sight. It was a contracted passenger jet from World Airlines. As we boarded the plane, there was euphoria that was indescribable. We were finally getting on transportation that would take us to "The land down under". As the plane cleared Vietnamese air space, a cheer went up. It was about a four-hour flight to Darwin, North Territories. During the flight, we had passes over Indonesia and numerous islands. As we touched down in Darwin, the Aussies on board screamed with delight. This was their native soil. We were given a custom form to fill out and a mini briefing. We were kept on board until an Australian official came and sprayed insect repellent down the aisle. Although this felt somewhat as a discourteous degradation, it was understandable. Finally, we got to leave and stretch our legs. As we walked to the terminal, a crowd of local onlookers clapped their hands and cheered us. What a wonderful feeling! This was a real pick-me-up. This was entirely different than the coldness and sometimes insults military people experienced at American airports. We had all been subjected to it and it was psychologically wounding.

Once inside, there was a world of friendly people. These included longhaired men, nice looking women and cold Victoria Bitter ale. There was much excitement in the air, as we knew that this was just a prelude to our week of R&R. Giddy and some that were alcohol infused, we boarded the plane again. Some of the grunts had to be helped. The flight to Sydney, New South Wales, took another four hours. The exceptional thing about the flight was the Australian desert and outback. I remember looking down and seeing a desolate, rusty orange, colored land, which was the nature of much of the continent. Most of the inhabitants live on or near the coast.

The touchdown in Sydney was filled with exuberant anticipation and yet another cheer. We were there! Everywhere you looked, were kangaroo, koala bear and native pictographs. Qantas, the main Australian airline, had kangaroos painted on the tails of their aircraft. On the bus, which drove on the left side of the road, we heard our first of many, "G'day mates." We were taken to the American R&R center to exchange money, get briefed and book our hotels. The American team had really done its homework. They gave us the do's and don'ts. We were told where to go if injured, emergency phone numbers and warnings. Apparently, there was a big, ongoing scam. American servicemen were being duped by cold and heartless con men into signing questionable contracts to buy real estate in Florida. Upon hearing this, everybody laughed. I thought, "Who could be that stupid?" As the briefing was going on, a beautiful, mini skirted young lady was wheeling around a money exchange cart. Although we heard much of what the briefer told us, she got most of the attention. There was a creator and heaven, because this was a walking, talking angel and had to be a harbinger of good things to come.

We had selected the Roosevelt Hotel. Friends who had been on R&R here earlier had recommended it. The mass of eager servicemen was broken down into hotel groups. There was another bus ride through downtown

Sydney to our hotel although the Roosevelt Hotel had seen better days; its appeal lay in its prominent, Victorian charm. The hotel manager was a pleasant, older lady. She recommended that we prepaid our hotel room and apart from daily spending money, put the rest in the hotel safe. This proved to be a very wise decision. It was at this point that I had the feeling of a bird locked in a cage with the door now being wide open. We flew out. Our military appearance and I.D. cards were a passport to the city. I had never met such friendly, open people in my entire life. Strangers became instant friends when they found out we were Americans, especially Southerners. Although Bill was a benign Yankee or "yank," as they called all of us, we made him an honorary, "family member." When we went to a pub, the tab was occasionally on the house. At restaurants, sometimes unknown admirers paid for our meals. This was a unique and unforgettable life experience. As the hotel manager had rightfully bragged, "Australian girls wear the shortest miniskirts in the world." Thereafter, we joyfully took the art of girl watching to a new plateau. It was glorious. On the first day to this temporary panacea, we had left a war, seen different countries and had a dream come true. That first day, we just oriented ourselves to our new emotions and surroundings. Acclimation took hold easily.

Steak dinners became part of our routine. The quality of the meat was superb. At the pubs were good old boys, instant "mates" and ale. This was a rough and tough, macho country. In almost every place and establishment, the men were the prime movers, and the women were separately bunched together. With a few receptive words, the dates were there. The women levitated toward American men, because I suppose, we treated them as equals and showed them a good time. In some cases, the girls openly competed against each other for our favor. The ego boost was in unfamiliar territory. People on the streets would come up to us and shake our hands because of our nationality. Many thanked us for the protection provided by our predecessors in World War II.

On one of our street outings, a grizzled older man, wearing a golf hat, walked up to us. He shifted his eyes side to side and then opened an overcoat. At first, we thought he was going to be a kinky "flasher," but this wasn't the case. "Aye mate, you wanna buy a watch?" We gawked in amazement. Both inside panels of his overcoat contained dozens of probably "hot" watches of all makes and sizes. A concerned passer-by sent him on his way, with a host of expletives. "Sorry about that mate. He's just a bum."

The most memorable street encounter startled off subtle and innocent. A pretty young lady approached us and asked us if we'd interested in some entertainment and free food. Of course, there was no question that we would go. We were led to a towering, modern, building and given a suite number to go to. In retrospect, it may have been the "El Alamein Hotel". When we got there, we found more American servicemen gathered. Their presence brought a great sense of security. We were seated at small tables in groups of two, with at least one well-dressed man. My host professed to be a Canadian. He seemed too friendly and too familiar. Club sandwiches and sodas were served. The live entertainment was a hula dance by pretty locals. As I looked around and behind me, I could see that the same thing was happening at each table. The doors that we had walked in through were now closed and locked. Standing at the door and prohibiting anyone from leaving was a huge, muscular man.

Something wasn't right there, and I became very uncomfortable. Suddenly, the room light went dim. A flickering light from a projector appeared, as well as a film. Very disconcerting and out of nowhere, a New Jersey accented voice announced, "F-F-F-F-Florida baby, that's where it's at!" It didn't take a rocket scientist to realize that this was a shakedown and the very same scam that we had been warned about. The words "And don't buy any land in Florida"' from the R&R orientation echoed in my head. Nobody was laughing now. I thought, "Oh my God, this isn't happening," but it was. I tried to remain calm but was really very anxious. The man giving the presentation went through his well-worn spiel about the "incredible" opportunities of buying land in Florida. Pictures of wholesome families having fun in the sun were shown. The smooth, honeyed voice of our plastic, smiling "agent" went on and on. These men were cold, professional con artists. The presentation was mesmerizing and almost hypnotic. Just as the presentation had started, without warning, it stopped and the room lights brightened. I was still adjusting my eyes when an incredibly fine printed contract was brought out and placed before me. A pen was shoved at my hand. "You really don't need to read it. This is a once in a lifetime opportunity. Don't be stupid," we were told. I told the demanding host that without proper consultation, I would not sign. His eyes, facial expressions and body language turned from warm, to glacial, intimidating and demeaning. A condescending berating followed. Having enough, I told him in no uncertain terms, that I was not interested. His condescension quickly evolved into overt, but incredibly controlled indignation.

This was shocking and I turned to make sure that my brother was not signing anything. There was a fleeting urge to get up on the stage and warn all the others about this scam. Incredibly, the New Jersey accented guy came to our table and told the Canadian ("closer") "We got a hot one"! This "hot one" was none other than our friend Bill. There was a last glare, then he went over to talk to Bill. Thankfully, he did not sign anything. we went over and got Bill, who was verbally jousting with the salesmen. Some in the audience had foolishly signed or were signing paperwork. Immediately upon signing, the documents were whisked away. Finally, a group of us got to the door and there was a standoff. However, when the odds became more in our favor and words were spoken, the big man yielded, and we rushed through the doors. I looked back, one last time. The con men were cleaning up all evidence, as fast as they could. I still have difficulty believing how unconscionable, callous and inhumane these people were. American servicemen were there seeking a respite from a terrible war, which had left its indelible mark on all of us. Yet, there were those who sought to victimize us, take advantage of our youth and inexperience and therefore exacerbate wounds. This incident was the only downside of the whole trip.

The attempted shakedown had rattled our cages. A warm pub and cold ale help settle our nerves. Later that night, we went to a popular place near Kings Cross called "The Cheetah Club." It was a young adult nightclub. Our military identification was the gold key that opened this door. There was live music and dancing. After being recognized as Americans, the beverages flowed freely and some of the girls waited in line to dance with eager servicemen. Two attractive ladies went back to the hotel with my brother and I. Bob was the odd man out. With no companion, he went back to his room in a stew. It was quite an evening. After my newfound friend had gone to sleep, I found myself up in Bill's room. The day's events had been an emotional roller coaster ride and talking to a comrade brought stabilization. Our rooms were several stories up and his was directly above mine. I eventually got tired. It was the wee hours of the morning, and I started back to my room downstairs. However, I discovered that I had left my key in my room, with the door locked. Now, I would either have to bang on my door or the managers door and wake someone up or rack out on Bills couch. With a friendly lady in my room, I was going to find a way to get back in my there, come hell or high water. There was only one other option to satisfy the conundrum. This would be to climb outside Bill's window and grab on to a large, metal, drainage pipe that went down the outside wall. I would then make my way down one story and get in through my outside window. At the time it seemed logical. When I lived in the Miami, Florida area as a young kid, tree climbing and jumping from limb to limb was second nature. We watched a lot of "Tarzan" on the black and white TV. It was up and down trees, nearly every day. In retrospect, it was not the most prudent of decisions and a long way to fall on unforgiving concrete, if I lost my grip. The window was opened, and the plan commenced. Bill was in awe and speechless.

It was cold outside, and the wind was blowing. As I eased out the window, I realized that the pipe was just out of reach. I jumped from the window ledge and caught and wrapped my hands around it. Looking down, I could see the hard concrete below me. Suddenly, the youthful foolishness of this enterprise dawned on me. There I was, dangling several stories up, outside a tall building, where I was only one slip from disaster. I would live through this or possibly not. Because of condensation on the pipe, I couldn't go back up and could only go down. I eased down to the level of my room window. I didn't even know if it was unlocked. My hands continued to slip. With one hand on the pipe and a foot on a pipe wall bracket, I leapt for the window ledge. After a momentary free fall, I managed to catch the ledge. Somehow, I made it. Luckily, my window was unlocked, but I had to hang on the bricked windowsill to get in. Once inside, I sat down and considered what had just transpired. The spontaneous plan had been quite literally "make or break" and unless there is an altered universe, I survived to relate the experience.

Out of the three of us, I alone had brought a camera. The remainder of our time was dedicated of sightseeing. We saw the Sydney harbor bridge and the famous opera building that had ongoing construction.

Our military I.D. cards got us into some more exclusive clubs. In every instance, we observed the men and women separated. The men were being good old boys and the women were sedate and conversing with each other. Whenever a man fell intoxicated, he was carried out accompanied with his female companion. These ladies followed expressionlessly, as if this were part of the accepted routine or modus operandi. It was our observation that "Sheila's", as they were called, seldom complained. When we chatted with the entourage of ladies, we were treated like long, lost, brothers. They encouraged us to have a good time and keep the ale coming. As a group, they promised to get us back to the hotel if they had to. We eventually made it back to our hotel and the nice warm beds. I do remember humor and laughter about the "mates."

The week went by too fast but will be forever stored in memory. We checked out of our hotel and assembled at the R&R center where we would be mustered out of country. Some on our original group didn't show up and were A.W.O.L. Although we couldn't condone their behavior, it was understandable. We, ourselves, were approached by hippies and asked if we wanted to stay. Some did. None of us wanted to return to the war. It was now time for us to return to the brutal reality we had originated from. Boarding our "freedom bird" to go back to "Nam" was agonizing. Most of us slept during the flight back. The pilot announced a specific island as we passed over it. I woke up to give it a brief glimpse and then went back to sleep. Landing back at Cam Ranh Bay, was a morale buster. The only redeeming factor was the fact that we were short timers. The R&R disbursement camp made us brush our teeth with some red-looking substance. This again felt dehumanizing and seemed that yet another notch was added in the distinct military degradation process. A C-130 military hop took us back to Tuy Hoa A.B. Then, the days would be counted off in earnest, until D.E.R.O.S. Departure back to the states where another "jungle" awaited us there.

Down Under

The heat of the day and peril of night gave way to a most benevolent flight.

The war behind and the land below, with portly sail, our craft would show.

Young hearts soared in wide-eyed wonder. Dreams came true in the land down under.

An unshaven face and skin with blotches, the old man came, to sell hot watches.

Up we went in a tower to travel, the wolves would prey on a misguided rabble.

Buy this land and the print was fine. The response was "Stuff, where the sun don't shine".

Our nerves were frayed and our faces pale. Bless their souls for Australian ale.

The night was full of flirting passes. We went home with Aussie lasses.

A key was locked in a room that night and a soul clung out on a drainage pipe.

Old friends would wait for thoughts to share. Back we flew to the dragon's lair.

An exotic war bore lambs to slaughter. It was trial by fire and flight over water.

First Tour Homecoming "Fire and Ice"

Just weeks after my nineteenth birthday, in November of 1968, I walked down an airplane ramp and was officially a combatant, in the Vietnam War. For me, virtually a child in a man's body, it was the beginning of "A world turned upside down". Now, a year later and mere weeks after my twentieth birthday, in November of 1969, I found myself presently walking up an airplane ramp that would expeditiously carry me away from this horrible quagmire. I was asking myself if this was merely a dream or just wishful thinking. The faces and excited body language of the other, American service members assured me that this was a real event. In the one year of combat duty, I had seen life and death and had filed away extraordinary memories. This tour of duty was ending, and I was returning "home". This was the day that I had dreamed about.

We buckled ourselves in, the engines revved up, we rolled down the runway and were up in the air. As we ascended, I couldn't help but worry about the enemy having one last opportunity to shoot our plane down and take us all out. What a propaganda "win" that would have been for them! However, this palpable malaise subsided, as our "freedom bird" rapidly gained altitude and soon crossed the coast. There was a cheer, when the announcement was made that we had cleared Vietnamese airspace. Now, the reality sunk in, we were at the commencement of crossing what we termed "The Pond". The "Fire" was now behind us. Our next stop would be Japan. After a few hours, we began our descent to Yokata Air Base, in the vicinity of Tokyo, Japan. We landed and pulled up to the terminal. It was great to get out and stretch our legs. We would be there just long enough for refueling and resupply. I went into a little gift shop and ended up getting some Japanese coins for souvenirs and a tangible memory of this, what was for me, a personal, historic event. We got back on our plane and took off again. Our next stop would be Anchorage, Alaska.

This was a long flight and many of us dozed off or chatted with fellow passengers. Finally, the announcement came that we were approaching Anchorage and we descended. Then touchdown, on American soil came with another loud cheer. Thank God, we made it back to our home country! As the plane rolled towards the terminal, we received an announcement that astonished me and I am sure, most of the other passengers. We were told that the airplane would not be rolling up to and connecting physically with the terminal. Instead, we would be parking what was determined to be a "safe distance" from it. This was due to the possibility of us bringing in and introducing some possible pathogen, contaminant or harmful insects.

Most of the service members, having come from a tropical climate, wore military clothing for that hot climate. Now, to get to the terminal, we would have to physically get to the ground outside, in the freezing weather. Otherwise, you could have stayed on the plane and that was of course, out of the question. As I got to the door, I could feel the freezing wind and it was a physical shock. Our bodies had acclimated to the tropical climate and besides this, we were not dressed for this cold weather. I can remember running to get inside and warm up. We were young and healthy, but this extreme temperature transition was brutal on our bodies.

It took time to warm up and stop shaking from the cold. Somehow, I found myself in a comfortable lounge. Now, I was going to have my first beer, on American soil, in over a year. I called the waitress over and ordered that precious, welcoming beer. A bottle of beer was put I front of me, but she asked me how old I was. I told her that I was twenty. She then gathered the unopened bottle of beer, so as to protect it and told me that I had to be twenty-one to legally consume alcohol there. I let her know that I had just gotten back from the war in Vietnam, but the answer was still "no"! This came as a complete and unexpected shock. I had just survived a year in a combat zone, a place where I could have easily been killed. However now, here in uniform, I was not old enough to drink a single beer. This was not the "welcome" that was expected and thankfully, the indignant anger was controlled.

We later returned/ ran back to our airplane and seated ourselves. One soldier was having a very difficult time. He was apparently so cold that he was shaking, and I do believe he was in the beginning stages of hypothermia, which could be life threatening. The stewardesses did their best to cover him with blankets and mercifully share body heat. This could have been any of us, including myself, and I felt considerable sympathy for him. In retrospect, I believe that he should have been taken to a hospital for observation and recovery, but he was not. The "Ice" was thankfully left behind, as we continued to the next stop of our very long journey. Our next stop was McGuire AFB, New Jersey. I believe that I eventually got a military hop (C-130 or C-141) to Charleston AFB, SC and "home". There was a month of decompression before I was introduced to Fairchild AFB, near Spokane, Washington. And then later to Myrtle Beach AFB, SC. Almost exactly a year after returning to the United States, I was given orders for yet another voluntary tour of Vietnam, in November of 1970. Prior to this, I had survived "Fire and Ice". Now, it was back to the "Fire" and yet more experiences and imbued memories.

An Education From The Bronx

I was very thankful to have survived my first year of combat duty in Vietnam and return safely, back to South Carolina. That year had been a very long and taxing one. We had transitioned from war zone to relative comfort zone. Now, I was back on familiar turf and surroundings, standing upright. I served the overseas tour with my brother, as we had signed up on the "buddy plan". That is, as an enlistment incentive, the USAF guaranteed that if you enlisted with a "buddy" you both would be together, throughout your enlistment. This was an easy way for them to get a twofer and more government inspected meat. I still have the newspaper clipping and photo of us with the USAF recruiter, in the local newspaper.

However, there had been a typical military snafu. At the end of our initial Vietnam tour, we got our next duty assignment orders. I had gotten an upcoming assignment to Fairchild AFB, in Washington state and my brother had gotten his for the much sought after, Myrtle Beach AFB, in South Carolina. Regardless, we were now both home recovering and acclimating, while our circumstance was being processed. The local congressional office had already been notified and was involved. I had gotten back in November of 1969, for thirty days of leave and had hoped that everything would be sorted out and I wouldn't have to go to the west coast and Washington. November turned into December and the only information from the congressional office was that they were still working on it. Nearing the end of my leave and Christmas just days away, I decided to call my receiving squadron, at Fairchild and request an extension of leave. I managed to get the First Sergeant and explained my request to him. He said that he understood, but they needed me up there asap.

Reluctantly, but obediently, I made the trip to Spokane, Washington, for duty at Fairchild AFB. It was a long, cross country flight and for the first time in my life, I was alone, with no family or friends. Once there, I made my way to the squadron offices and checked in. It all just seems like a blur now, with so many things that had to be done. At last, I got a barracks and room assignment. It was good to hit the rack and rest. Within a day or so after my arrival, I got a roommate. His name was "Richard" and he was from the Bronx. I didn't know it at the time, but although unsought, I was in for a very interesting, education.

Richard was a loquacious individual, whose thick Bronx accent just begged to be listened to. We both went down to the accounting and finance office to arrange payment for our meals, at the chow/dining hall. There were a couple of ways to do this. One option was to get paid a monetary amount, for all three meals, every month, while the other option was to get an immediate, paper "meal card". This meal card was presented, at entry and entitled the holder to dine, after the appropriate sign in. I always got the meal card, because no matter if I had run out of money, I was always entitled to any meal and all I could eat. However, Richard, on the other hand, opted to be paid monthly for meals. The problem with this was that yes, everyone in this program was indeed paid for all meals, on our monthly payday. However, some service members would always run out of money and had none to pay for their meals, at the end of the month. Usually, the married airmen chose to be paid monthly for their meals, due to dining with their families mostly. Occasionally individuals would inquire as to why I got a meal card versus being paid monthly and usually in a condescending manner, while sometimes smirking. It was a version of the old "crab pot" mentality. This is a metaphor, with respect to a collective thought or "group think". In essence, this is "we" believe our thought is the only one that counts. Any individual thought counter to this is subordinate, irrelevant and unwise. "They" would always come up with, "Are you going to eat every meal, every day in the chow hall?". My comeback was always about the ability to get meals without payment. It would never fail that one of these critics would typically run out of money before payday and would meekly ask to use my meal card or someone else's to get food. I would usually oblige, but getting caught doing this would mandate confiscation of my card. Sometimes those that borrowed my card thanked me, sometimes they didn't. As it turned out, one of the critics of me getting a meal card, Richard, ran out of money before payday, as I had earlier predicted.

I woke up one morning, via a mental, proximity alert. This was deeply imbued and acquired in Vietnam, for personal survival. Apparently, my desperate roommate was attempting to surreptitiously remove the dimes that I had inserted into the tops of my civilian loafer-shoes. When I asked what he was doing, he awkwardly told me that he was out of money and was hungry. Instead of escalating this into a confrontation, I suggested that we both go back to the personnel center and get him switched out to a meal card. He acquiesced and we immediately went to the finance and accounting section. He stepped in and explained his situation to the first available clerk we came across. Although sympathetic, the clerk told him that he had already been paid for all his meals for that current month and could only get a meal card for the beginning of the next month. Richard started to get agitated and again plead his case. The clerk then suggested for him to get an emergency loan to sustain him through the end of the month. It was apparent that this clerk had heard this redundant story, all too often. Yes, and from all those clever ones in the "crab pot" that knew it all, but really didn't. In a moment of anguished dismay, Richard had what I can only describe as a reactive catharsis or "Bronx comeback". With his hands extended out and palms upward, he looked at me and exclaimed with unfeigned, animated injury, "Get a loan, he says!".

What is not in doubt is that the clerk and me were not the only eyes and ears that were privy to this brief, but very entertaining soliloquy. He and his colleagues surely must have also welcomed some color, interjected into their usually monotonous, type written, black and white world. It could have even precipitated a timely, after work "beer call". This unchoreographed, indelible performance was indeed unforgettable. However, distraught, he did not apply for the suggested, emergency loan. Instead, I took care of my roommate, until he was able to finally get his own meal card. For this unexpected acte de gentillesse, Richard and I became good friends, and he opened up about his personal life, before the military and the Bronx. We would have more interesting adventures together.

Fairchild AFB was a SAC or Strategic Air Command base. Its primary mission was to provide the U.S. with a nuclear weapons strike capacity and deterrent, via its squadron of B 52 bombers. Prior to going to Vietnam, I was at another SAC base at Westover AFB, in Massachusetts for a year. The missions of both were similar.

We, as security policemen, were tasked with the physical protection of these vital, strategic assets. While at Westover, three of us got a pass and bus tickets for an introductory visit to the big apple, NYC. It was astonishing, eye opening and just another world altogether. The enormity of the venue and complexity of the experience was all consuming. It was analogous to being like a few ants in a giant, populated ant hill. And I can say with a fair degree of certainty that It was probably obvious to all we met, in this street wise metropolis, that we were fish out of water.

I had been told that my thirty-day leave could not be extended, prior to singing in, because I was needed asap. However, the facts on the ground were considerably different. Because it was Christmas time, our mandatory, incoming training was delayed, for much of the holidays. This also validated the old military gripe of "Hurry up and wait". I could have easily had time to stay home a few more days and enjoy the holidays there, instead of hanging around the barracks, just passing time. However, I was able to get educated about life in New York City from my roommate.

Richard kept me enthralled, with his articulate, city knowledge and personal experiences. I learned of the five boroughs of New York City and too many insider stories to remember. He was from a working-class Jewish family, but I never observed him to be a conformant to this faith. You would have never known, unless he told you. He had also been told that his mother was deceased, at an early age and that one of his sisters was in a long term, mental facility. However, we were to get a call in the barracks one day, which I answered that was quite shocking. His brother called from NYC and requested to talk to Richard. I went and got him, and they chatted for a while. When he returned to our room, he appeared confused and shocked. His brother had discovered that the mother they thought was deceased, was in fact placed in possibly the same mental facility as their sister. Her condition was apparently pronounced. This news affected him noticeably. As a very young adult, with little world experience, there was no way for me to adequately console this suffering friend. When he was finally able to discuss this with me, he said that it all made sense to him now. The family and extended family has been somewhat secretive, and some things weren't talked about and was therefore puzzling. His mother's severe mental health and disposition had been kept from the children to shield them. Now, the final piece of the puzzle was in place and everything that had transpired made sense. It was very sad, and it was a meaningful, but melancholy life experience.

December of 1969 had now passed, and it was January of 1970. There was snow, ice and a deep, permeating coldness. With everyone back from their holiday leave, the training could now begin, in earnest. Our barracks was a considerable distance from the training facility, so we usually had to walk there in the extreme weather. I had a car, but it was back in SC. Transportation was an issue and walking there was misery.

The idea eventually came up of acquiring a cheap, used car, which were always being sold, on the base. People had old cars, when they had to leave, they would sell them cheaply. With the disposition of my orders, relocating me to Myrtle Beach pending and already having a car, it made no sense for me to get another one. So, Richard found a running, old car and bought it. However, there was a conundrum to this perceived panacea. He did not have either a driver license or was he able to pay additionally for car insurance. No longer wanting to walk, in the frigid weather, I came up with an ad hoc suggestion. I could be the primary driver and if we had any issue with being stopped, accident etc. while he was driving, we could switch places. This is provided there was time to do this and was an urgent need. This worked for a while. Richard got pulled over for a traffic violation once and the base cop was right behind us. The was no time to switch out. The cop found out that we were fellow policemen and let us go. On another occasion, Richard was driving too fast for conditions. He spun out on the ice and into a fixed, metal object. He then panicked and asked me to switch places. As the car was still drivable, it was late at night and there were no witnesses, I strongly suggested that the best course of action was for us to just leave, with all expediency. Even if we had needlessly switched places, the result would have been the same. He begrudgingly did and it made us both reflect. I believed that it would just be a matter of time before his unskilled driving, with no driver's license or insurance was going to place us both into an untenable position. And, for both of us, there was always the issue of "switching places". Although the old car bought us a few welcome weeks of "out of the cold weather" transportation, it just didn't work out. However, we were eventually able to hook up with another New Yorker that had a car. This experience lent credence to the old adage about the need and benefit of having connections. In retrospect, I believe that car ownership and the ability to drive that personal property was an aspirational desire for a poor kid from the Bronx. That box was now checked.

Now, with the car debacle over, a source of friction and loss of trust between my roommate and me was removed. The big elephant in the room was now gone. We started over as friends and had begun to swap stories again. Because of the dynamics of his origins, his tales were usually very interesting. As I said previously, Richard was from working class, Jewish family, in the Bronx. There was a certain degree of penury in this unorthodox and atypical family.

Coeur d’Alene, Idaho

The one winter of duty that I spent at Fairchild was a very slow moving, gut every hour out, grind. Our jobs were to be outside in the weather and physically guard the nuclear uploaded, B-52’s. The cold winds blowing down from Canada could be relentless. There were times that I thought that I was going to get permanent damage from frostbite and times that I wanted to just give up and go to some place that was warm. Some others did break down and do this. Furthermore, when it got too cold, the K-9 dogs were removed from the elements, out of concerns for their health and safety. We were not and it was misery. My roommate and I were going to have to do something memorable with our time off, to break the monotony and keep our sanity in check. So, when we were going to have a few days off, we decided to hitch hike to Coeur d'Alene, Idaho, in the middle of the winter. This was out of a sense of adventure, monotony and the naivety of youth. For whatever reason, it seemed like a good idea, at the time. There was no problem getting out of the base and onto the main road. With our military bearings and short haircuts, it was obvious that we were military guys. The culture and style of the time was that the local, civilian men had long hair and sometimes beards. This was especially true, out on the west coast. Because of the current anti-war sentiments, there was occasional unpleasantness towards military personnel. However, in this situation, it worked in our favor. We were able to get continuous pickups and drop offs. Many of the rides were from WW2 veterans. We arrived in Coeur d'Alene, in the early evening. This was fresh territory for us. I do remember us walking by a high school that was having some kind of dance. We paid an entry fee and walked in and checked it out. We were obviously older than the kids, who were mostly paired up. So, we just stayed a short while and left. We eventually ended up at a location that was very friendly and accommodating.

Satisfied that our quest to have a successful adventure was accomplished, we began our return back. However, it was late at night and the cars were just not appearing. We did manage to get one ride that dropped us off, some distance from town and at a very snow-covered intersection. We thanked the individual for the ride and then waited for another car that did not come. Except for distant, stationary lights, it was just us, darkness and cold. Not having any luck, we decided to walk for a while, in what we believed was the right direction. There was just the sound of our feet crunching snow, again the darkness, muted conversation and the bitter cold. The hours passed and we saw no one. We were both exhibiting signs of hypothermia. I don't know what Richard's thoughts were, but mine were as dark as the night, which presently enveloped us. With the now continuous snowing, it was difficult to make out almost any point of reference. It was at times, a "white out". I truly believed that we were going to freeze to death, at a nowhere place, here in Idaho. Maybe someone would find our bodies, after the spring thaw or maybe not. Wild things in nature have to eat good and the military fed us well. Possibly, upon our demise, there would even be memorial marker, by some thoughtful entity. It just got bitterly colder, as the wind gusts blew. I believe that we both had nearly given up hope. However, maybe it was my hopeful imagination, but I believed that I noticed a very slow-moving pair of headlights, in the distance. We waived our arms, as the lights continued to approach and eventually came to a stop. It was an individual, Idaho police officer, making a routine, winter sweep and it was a life saver.

He listened to our harrowing story and then kindly took us to an area motel, where we spent the night. The motel was a low budget, out of the way place, but for us, it was the Taj Mahal. And to be warm once again was so wonderful and satisfying. I woke up the next morning, to the glory of sunlight I thought I might never see again and a loud burst of rumbling flatulence, from a snickering Richard. Because of his difficult and sometimes tumultuous upbringing, for him, this adventure had been just water off a ducks' back. However, for me it was indelible. Since it was our last day off, we got a quick breakfast and were able to hitch hike successfully back to our base and barracks. We went to work the next day, on time, a little more mature and still kicking.

Spring finally came, the snow and ice melted, and we were able to enjoy many of the sights, sounds and personal developments, through the broad prism of the "Great Northwest Experience". Although there were other friendships and exploits, the ones that I have here so articulated, were the most memorable. Richard got orders for Vietnam, and I finally got mine to Myrtle Beach. The return flight home from Spokane, Washington was an equally long one, but welcome. I rejoined my brother at Myrtle Beach AFB, and it was so much better than my previous assignment. I had been only there for a short period, when I got called in for an interview by the OSI or USAF Office of Special Investigation. I was presented with a copy of a letter that had been written by Richard, from Vietnam to his New York friend from Fairchild. Apparently, they had a dialogue about the use of marijuana. He also went on to talk about the adventures that he and I had. Since my name was mentioned, they wanted to know if I had any additional information about his/their marijuana use.

In our barracks at Fairchild, some had easy access to marijuana and there was at times the acrid scent of its use and residue. There was one fellow police sergeant that we believed was lifer material. He always wore a starched and pressed uniform and had spit shined shoes. As a potential career man (lifer), no one would ever expect that he had a possibly malfeasant alter ego, as a drug dealer. One day, I was in my barracks room alone and there was a knock on my door. This potential career man asked to come in and chat. He had with him what looked to be an expensive briefcase. Not batting an eye, he opened this briefcase. And inside of it were numerous, well-packed packages of what appeared to be marijuana. Completely caught off guard and shocked, I declined purchasing. He left and possibly greeted another potential client. There is always the possibility that this was a sting, given his observed nature.

Anyway, I was unable to give the OSI any more information than they already had, and it was obvious that they were closing in on a solid case. I never found out what eventually transpired. Unfortunately, Richard was never one of those that benefited from an overabundance of good luck. However, I was at Myrtle Beach through the fall and eventually returned to Vietnam, in November of 1970.

Part Two Bien Hoa AB, Republic of Vietnam

The Metamorphosis

Law Enforcement

Towards the end of boot camp at Lackland AFB, Texas, job assignments were given out. About half of our boot camp flight were to be trained as security policemen. While the other half were given other, various assignments. There was, at the time, a great need for USAF military policemen. This was because of the ongoing war in Vietnam. This specialty was bifurcated into security or law enforcement. The training of this specialty was by either a school or by direct duty assignment (DDA) and on the job training (OJT). Inevitably, my brother and I were sent DDA to Westover AFB, Mass. We both arrived a few days after Christmas, in 1967. There was snow everywhere and it was intensely cold. This was a B-52 bomber base and hence, a part of the Strategic Air Command (SAC). Here, we provided security for the bombers that carried nuclear weapons. Most of this duty consisted of physically guarding these war machines, outside in the elements and on our feet, for 8-12 hours. Even with our raw youth and being former athletes in high school, it was a daily challenge, just to make it through these shifts. Some did not make it. There was one "accidental" Russian roulette death; at least one airman going "section 8" (nuts) on a personnel post and a few that couldn't take it anymore and just walked off of their freezing posts. These are some of the incidents that I am aware of. The dynamics of this hardship were very challenging.

Orders for Tuy Hoa AB, Republic of Vietnam, came with welcomed relief. I arrived in November of 1968, with my brother arriving a week or so later, due to an administrative issue. We were both assigned to the prestigious Tiger Flight (security). After this first tour was completed, I was sent to Fairchild AFB (SAC), Washington and again dispensed to provide security for nuclear loaded, B-52 bombers. Reiterating, my brother was assigned to Myrtle Beach AFB, SC ahead of me. This was a Tactical Air

Command (TAC) base, with tactical jet fighters. After a few months, I eventually linked back up with him at Myrtle Beach AFB, SC, where the assignment was law enforcement and actual, military cop duty. Towards the end of the year, we were both given orders to work in law enforcement again, at Bien Hoa (Been Wah) AB, Republic of Vietnam. The air force bases (AB) in Vietnam were under the Pacific Air Command (PACAF). I arrived back in Vietnam, in November of 1970. I would go on to serve two tours of duty there, as a law enforcement specialist.

The Job

The military complex at Bien Hoa was sprawling. Bien Hoa Air Base was virtually a self-sustaining city. It consisted of a main fighter wing, with the usual support and accommodating infrastructure. We shared the base with and were guests of an associated VNAF (Viet Nam Air Force) wing and its components. The air base was split up into an American side and a Vietnamese side. The American side had an army special forces unit and an "Air America" compound. We all knew that Air America was a cover for the CIA. It had to be one of the worst kept secrets of the war.

The Vietnamese side was the larger of the two. There was never any doubt what country ran the show, with the Vietnamese being a convenient façade. Some of the lucky Vietnamese servicemen were housed with their families there. This base also served as a basic training site for those fortunate enough to be chosen for duty, in the VNAF. Most eligible Vietnamese men were drafted for the army ARVN) Army of the Republic of Vietnam). Prior to being inducted into the service, each was given an exam. Those that scored high enough were given aa choice for the relative safety of the national air force or navy. Those slots were highly sought after, since military duty in the armed services was in essence, for the duration of the war. Service in the national army or marines was often a one-way ticket and it was survival of the luckiest. The indigenous forces had an ongoing AWOL problem, with many of these individuals simply trying to mitigate their misfortune.

Adjoining the air base and sharing a gate was Bien Hoa Army Base, home of the 1st Air Cavalry Division. Their shoulder patch emblem was triangular shaped. It had a yellow background; a black line ran diagonally from top to bottom and the head of a black horse was in one of its corners.

These were well trained, persistent and ferocious soldiers. These ground pounding warriors were helicoptered in and out of hot spots and were given the nickname “grunts”. Like the ARVN, which they justifiably had little respect for, the grunts had the worst going of it and some of the highest field mortality rates. Their workhorse was the UH-1 Huey helicopter. This was the first turbine helicopter to enter combat production. They were painted drab army green and anyone in this combat theater knew their audible “chop, chop, chop” meant business. Here, these platforms were called “chopper” for a good reason. This is one of the permeated sounds that I still remember and sometimes hear in thoughts and dreams.

A few miles down the road, between Bien Hoa and Saigon was long Binh. If the military complex at Bien Hoa was big, Long Binh would be gigantic. It was a staging area and a war material depot. It also had some notoriety as home of Long Binh Jail or as it was more commonly referred to as LBJ. If one was unfortunate enough to be sent to LBJ, then you had some real problems. Being in USAF law enforcement, I had on occasions apprehended individuals who had broken military law. This was the Uniform Code of Military Justice or UCMJ. Some of these individuals ultimate, in country destination became LBJ. We heard rumors about LBJ and its comparison to the military prison facility at Ft. Leavenworth, Kansas. I was told that the latter was nicer; at least it had stateside accommodations.

As law enforcement specialists, we were assigned both gate and patrol duty. The Bien Hoa main city gates were the water tower gate and was manned by two USAF and two VNAF policemen. This was the primary U.S. ingress/ egress gate. The other city gate was the Vietnamese gate. It was manned by two VNAF and one USAF policeman. The traffic here was primarily Vietnamese military and civilians. The army gate, as we called it was army and air force traffic and it was manned by one USAF and one USA military policeman. There was another gate on the VNAF side that was always manned by at least two VNAF policemen. This gate was periodically manned by an additional USAF policeman, depending on available manpower.

This was remote and was abutted by a nearby rice paddy and had a long access road. I would have unforgettable experiences, at each of these gates.

The patrols were mostly law enforcement, with at least one exception. This exception was a heavily armed, joint allied, security patrol. It usually consisted of one USAF and two VNAF policemen. This was in a U.S.

military jeep armed with a belt fed M-60 machine gun. We had side arms and one or more M-16 rifles. The American serviceman was the team leader. On occasions, there would be static postings e.g. base exchange (BX), bank, etc. The Vietnamese civilians all knew about the much sought after and rationed goodies, in what they annunciated the "Be-ek". The base exchange was the usual epicenter for military-civilian, black marketing and corruption.

Although the USAF was supposed to be the best qualified and scrutinized service, we had to deal with some unsavory dregs of our finite society. Each of us in this specialty constituted a thin line against military and civilian misconduct and corruption. We were authorized to use up to deadly force, if necessary. The problems with policing our community, were exacerbated by poor attitudes of non-career members, and visiting grunts, working on deaths doorstep. Much of our time was spent correcting uniform violations, issuing traffic citations and chasing down drug pushers and users. Theft, prostitution and black-market activities were trouble spots, with respect to the Vietnamese. There was also the sensitive subject of racial strife, within our ranks of service members. Although our presence and purpose were to present a unified front against a common adversary, sometimes we were our own, worst enemy. Ultimately, the drug problem became so severe; we had to sometimes subordinate marijuana sellers/ users, to concentrate on the apex drug heroin, and its malevolent tentacles.

During my first tour of duty, the Vietnamese people and their dissimilar ways were so "foreign", that many of us American service members thought that they were analogous to being people from a different planet. They dug through our garbage, ate strange smelling and looking food, had their own mannerisms and in general, it was just a big culture shock. However, just as a school student realizes, what you don't know or understand sometimes produces a negative perception. At this juncture, I decided to learn all about the people and their culture that were recipients of our country's blood and treasure.

Again, Vietnam emerged as a distinct civilization during the first milium B.C. It was conquered by China, during the Han dynasty and under Chinese rule for one thousand years. In A.D. 939, the Vietnamese restored their independence and expanded southward along the coast of the South China Sea, from their historic epicenter, in China's Red River Valley. In the nineteenth century, Vietnam was conquered once again and subjugated and absorbed with Cambodia and Laos, into French Indochina and French colonial rule. After World War II, communists led Viet-Minh guerillas fought for several years to gain independence. Subsequently, the French were soundly defeated in the battle of Dien Bien Phu in 1954 and a long span of French rule came to an end. In 1954, at the Geneva conference, the country was divided into a communist North Vietnam and a non-communist South Vietnam. With unification as the goal, the North, led by Ho Chi Minh, prosecuted a war against the south. This war came to be known to the world as the "Vietnam War". In Vietnam, it is called the "American War".

The French colonized Indochina, in great part, so they could exploit the abundant natural resources. They built the infrastructure, much of what exists today. Their European trained engineers professionally built roads, bridges and modernized cities. Their scholars meticulously took the Chinese characterized alphabet and westernized it. French priests spanned across the country. Their missionaries came and converted the masses to the catholic church. Presently, Catholicism is second to Buddhism. The French legal system was introduced and adapted. French food and drink were added to the Vietnamese diet. The French also left their mark in another way. Their Eurasian offspring were both handsome men and beautiful women.

Historically, there were many famous and legendary Vietnamese kings and queens. A bigger than life statue of King Tran Hung Dao

(c. AD 1229-AD 1300), on a mounted stallion was near Saigon harbor. His face was on the watermark of the South Vietnamese currency. His ferocity, tenacity and cunning victories in battles against the mostly and overwhelming Chinese enemy were legendary. There were the two queen sisters, Hai Ba Tru'ng (c. AD 14-AD 43). Rather than surrender to an overwhelming hostile enemy, they defiantly jumped from a bridge into the Hat-Giang River and drowned themselves. This bravery and extraordinary act of patriotism rallied the people.

Indigenous songs and plays have been written about their ancestors and they are fiercely proud of this heritage. The more that I learned about the culture and history of Vietnam, the closer I got to the people. It made me realize that they were just like us, in many ways and fellow human beings. There was much common ground to develop upon.

As I alluded to earlier, the air base at Bien Hoa was a joint use base. The VNAF had their side and the Americans had theirs. We had joint allied security and law enforcement patrols. I requested to be put on as many of these joint patrols as possible, to befriend the Vietnamese servicemen and learn firsthand, about them. I struck up many friendships and saw many of my new comrades as possible. The Vietnamese were extremely receptive and appreciative. I assimilated with them. I learned their language as best I could and adopted as many mannerisms as practical and possible. Most other American servicemen did not go into the development of likewise relationships. However, what I was doing started to rub off and attitudes began to change. As the Vietnamese came to know me, I became popular with them. Even though they had little money, they would sometimes take me out to lunch, on the Vietnamese side. I was usually the only American, in these crowded cafes. There are times that I felt that I was the first American some of them had seen at these venues. For them, it was astonishing that an American would not only be there, but also eat with them and consume their cuisine. My hosts were especially proud when I broke out the chopsticks and used them like a native. However, there were times when I felt like an observed animal in the zoo. Small crowds would sometimes actually gather nearby, to watch me eat. Sometimes when I finished a meal, I was applauded, and hands went out to shake or just touch. It was something else. On several occasions, I offered to pay, but was never allowed to. Also, the VNAF cops on our joint patrols didn't have a chow break, but we did. I wanted to change that. So, with me, I started giving them chow breaks and then it caught on. On occasion, individuals told me that they were hungry, but didn't have any money. I gave them the money, as the cost was very cheap. The gesture was appreciated.

There is one final, memorable and related episode that I wish to convey. One day, I happened to have Bien Hoa city gate duty with a higher ranking VNAF NCO. This individual was known to be sometimes cold and distant towards his American counterparts. Upon arriving for duty this day, he seemed to be in a state of obvious melancholy.

I came to find out that a young daughter of his was seriously ill. A prognosis for a quick recovery was questionable, if he did not get some expensive medication, which he could not afford. He eventually wrote down the name of the medication and gave it to me. I just happened to be good friends with a supervisor, at our clinic/ dispensary. I was soon able to go by there and asked my friend for a favor, as I explained the situation. He left briefly and returned with a container of the needed medication. I immediately went back to the city gate and placed this medication in the man's hand. He appeared to be caught completely off guard. From this empathetic gesture, there was a great level of expressed appreciation, and a solid bond was established. Word spread and although access to the city was limited to a few American servicemembers, I would thereafter have unfettered access through that city gate and all the adventures that awaited.

Furthermore, I was now one of them and was likewise shown considerable respect. The relative metamorphosis had now been brought to fruition. I was no longer the lowly crawling caterpillar, but rather a fully developed butterfly. This evolution was a very gratifying consequence.

Evolution

From germination to termination, our bodies grow and learn.
Across our land, across the world, the flame of hope does burn.

Liberty and equality are paths we must pursue.
Communication is the key in everything we do.

To speak our tongues or others, there are words we must rehearse.
The great cultures of the world are many and diverse.

The caterpillar crawls the ground, oblivious to the world.
It changes to a butterfly, with legs and wings unfurled.

Different peoples of the earth join us, take your place.
We're all one bonded entity, it's called the huma race.

Battle Damage

Usually when I went on patrol, I never knew what might transpire during that particular watch. So, I was on a law enforcement patrol one day, when I heard on the radio that a jet fighter was coming in, with heavy battle damage. Furthermore, a copilot was also badly wounded. Not knowing exactly what shape the crew or aircraft was in, I raced to the flight line. The firetruck and other emergency vehicles were already there, with emergency lights on. Out of my distant left, a Cessna A-37 Dragonfly started its approach. As it descended and closed, I could see that something was dreadfully wrong. The overhead canopy was missing and one of the pilots, seated in this side-by-side aircraft was leaning forward and appeared to be unconscious. When they touched down, it was obvious that this jet had been in a battle. The pilot operating this craft had done a real professional job bringing it back safely. It taxied off the runway and onto the flight line, where it eventually stopped. There was another approaching jeep filled with "on call" pilots that sped past me, to the center of attention. They did not heed my flashing red light to stop and went straight to the plane. This had been one of theirs and emotions were running high. The one viable pilot got help lifting his wounded comrade out of the cockpit and onto the ground. When the man's helmet was removed, it was apparent that he was already deceased and that I had just seen a dead pilot brought in from his last flight. The aircraft had been hit through the bottom, by enemy groundfire. This killed the copilot and had also taken off their canopy.

The initial information stated that were "two souls onboard". However, one of the souls had already departed and in doing so, just left its earthly vessel behind. This was depressing and heartbreaking. When his body was inevitably taken away, the fire truck crew hosed down the bloody mess on the pavement. Sadly, we all knew that across the pond and back home, his unknowing family was sure to be worried about him. Subsequently, there would soon be an official visit to his next of kin and their world would be broken forever. I don't believe that any of us that witnessed this sad event could sleep very well for a few days, afterwords.

There were a few controlled crashes I observed, where the runway was foamed, and dysfunctional fighter jets carefully landed into this solution. Every time, sparks flew out, upon contact. There was a very audible metal on concrete scraping sound, until the aircraft slid to a complete stop. Once, there was a deadly crash, at the opposite end of the runway, where the pilot came in short, and he died. The burned aircraft remnants were there for some time, before they were cleaned up and removed. A memorial service was held at our base chapel for him. Each one of these somber services was always one too many.

There was one occasion, where I was on an allied patrol with two other VNAF policemen. We were in proximity to the army gate, when an A1E Skyhawk in trouble, had to make an emergency landing. As soon as I spotted the descending aircraft, I turned the jeep in its direction. This was a VNAF prop fighter that probably still had some ordinance aboard. The friction sparks started flying as he hit the runway surface. We were almost on him when it stopped sliding. I got out and ran to the side of the cockpit to assist the pilot, as he exited. He was eventually able to unhook his harness, slide the canopy back and exit. Then we both rapidly returned to the jeep. As it still had that ordinance on it, I immediately removed us all from the area to a safe distance. The pilot, a captain, seemed to be shaken up by the close call, as we all were. We sat there for a while, and he began quickly discussing something with the two VNAF security people. The gist of the discussion was that he wanted to return back to the wreck immediately. They went back and forth, but I eventually put the jeep in gear, and we all returned. He then got out and ran to the cockpit where he retrieved a catholic rosary and an apparent photograph of his young family. These were personal items that he had held great value in and which apparently accompanied him on his dangerous missions. We could have been seriously wounded or worse from an ordinance explosion, but thankfully, this did not happen. He was a handsome man, with a nice-looking family. He now had his tangible representations of his faith and family safely with him and I completely understand his rationale. We had all dodged a potential bullet and it had been worth the risk.

Scene of The Grime

"Ronnie" as I will articulate, for this story, will always and forever be, the infamous and legendary "GRMT" (pronounced grimt). This acronym was coined by my good-natured friend "Wally", a big kid of Serbian descent from the Cleveland, Ohio area. The "GRMT" stood for Goofy gums, Rotten roots, Musky molars and Tired teeth. "Ronnie" aka "The GRMT" was a raunchy serviceman from New England and he spoke with a Massachusetts, accented lisp. He was undoubtedly, the grubbiest serviceman that I had met, to that point in my life. He rarely bathed and we were all working in the unmerciful heat and humidity of the tropics. His hair was always greasy, speckled with dandruff and stank. In retrospect, I believe that if he somehow disappeared in a body of water, rescuers would only have to look for an oil slick, to locate his corpse. His offensive body odor was like a mixture of chopped onions, dried sweat and grunge. The most prominent attribute was his dental hygiene or lack thereof.

He had one finicky and nasty routine. He would buy new packs of underwear and undershirts from the Base Exchange. Subsequently, he would periodically change into new underclothing and wear them until they were completely filthy. When this indiscriminate point came to pass, he would just toss the old underclothing and put on a new pair, without showering. I think this was the particularly egregious habit that bothered us, in our barracks, the most.

When he talked, the darkened, jagged and decaying teeth were obvious. Food particles, old and new were visible and stuck between plaque covered teeth. I remember all "GRMT" veterans having to talk to him at an angle, to deflect and avoid the malodorous, overpowering breath. It is still an unanswered mystery of how he ever passed the physical examination to get into the USAF. I believe that had he ever gargled with hydrogen peroxide, in this condition, his mouth would have exploded with fizz.

Perhaps the CIA might have better harnessed his "biohazard" attributes. They could have threatened captured prisoners to give up information. Otherwise, they would have been tethered to Ronnie for a long period of time. Since Vietnam was a proxy battle in the cold war, it was even possible that the KGB could have kidnapped and turned Ronnie and subsequently used him for the same adversarial purposes, in a dark, Soviet gulag.

Ronnie just appeared one day and reported to the barracks chief, me, as a replacement. I don't believe that he ever had a roommate, which was indeed fortunate. Reaction to his obvious condition was immediate and universally negative. Off duty, he sequestered himself in his cubicle, didn't go out very often and had no friendships with colleagues that I am aware of. In the barracks, he was insulted and demeaned mercilessly and often. Fellow airmen sometimes tossed toothpaste, toothbrushes, bars of soap and antiperspirants over his door and into his cubicle. The most common taunts were, "Hey, Ronnie, wash your stinking ass!" or "Brush your f*****g teeth!" Apparently, he was hardened to his lifestyle and the prodding was useless and of no consequence. Oddly enough, he was somehow, ultimately introduced to captain "John" the army pilot, that I had flown with on occasion. On one of these missions with John, the ordinance was fired off and I still have permanent hearing loss and ringing ear from it.

I can only guess that there was some kind of misfit chemistry between them. Perhaps theirs was a fellowship of oddballs and outcasts and it mercifully took the pressure off of us. Eventually, we observed Ronnie wearing an army flight suit. No doubt, this had come from his adventures with John. Although these missions were probably unauthorized, Ronnie began boasting of his newfound, albeit unlawful exploits. No one was going to rat him out, because no matter what we thought of him, he was one of us and it was always us against the lifers. Since I had also had a few unauthorized flights with John and highly respected by my contemporaries, the escapades were muted. However, this "in your face" boasting came to an abrupt end, due to a marital incident. We all knew that Ronnie was married, but we couldn't fathom what kind of woman could ever tolerate or bring herself to marry this insufferable, malodorous, deviant.

In a true testament to the checks and balances of life and the natural law of reciprocity, karma would intercede on our behalf. My friend Wally was a gifted sketch artist and eventually found himself at work, as the squadron "illustrator". It was here: in the back offices of the "cop shop" that he discovered an intelligence coup. This astonishing discovery developed into a full-fledged catharsis.

Out of the blue, from reliable sources, came various stories of Ronnie getting a dreaded, “Dear John” letter from home. Extraordinary and forthcoming things were amiss. This was validated by Wally, who had fortuitously found the fantabulous and fascinating “mother lode”. One day, in his duties as squadron illustrator, he found the actual “Dear John” correspondence that Ronnie had gotten. In this was a photograph, worth its weight in gold and precious gems. The treasurable photograph showed a picture of Ronnie’s wife and another man, naked in their marital bed, at home. Both of them were smiling and each had one hand raised, giving the camera and him specifically “The Finger”. The news of this wonderful and astonishing discovery spread like a windblown, prairie wildfire. This was a profoundly jubilant and historical moment. The perpetrators perfidious and provocative act providentially, provided us with a profound cornucopia of phenomenal joy and harmonic ecstasy. However, another question arose and was considerable food for thought. “Who…the…hell…took…the …picture”? As the glorious information spread, the story rapidly evolved, with assorted versions and became more convoluted and baser. The inevitable domestic train wreck had been brought to fruition. There was…a God in heaven. Payback was legendary, .and it was gloriously imbued with gratifying magnificence.

Ronnie’s inglorious and inevitable exit out of the squadron was primarily facilitated by a self-inflected wound, from an accidental shooting.

He was on one of the gates and began playing “quick draw cowboy”. He had impulsively done this a few times, at work and in my presence; it had made the Vietnamese police and me very uneasy. I made him stop. However, out of my sight and presence, the old habit apparently came back. One time when he holstered his .38 pistol, during this dangerous game, the hammer was pulled slightly back and it then “popped a cap”. The bullet went down his leg. Already being an eschewed reprobate, it landed him in some very hot water. The military didn’t take kindly to this very dangerous recklessness, from someone in such a position of authority. Instead of an honorable purple heart, he got a well deserved, purple shaft.

Much to our relief, he wasn’t in our ranks, very long after that incident. The preponderance of the accumulated indiscretions had become intolerable.

After the dust settled somewhat, I recall seeing Ronnie with a new and complete set of dentures. Being used to the old Ronnie, he was almost unrecognizable. Apparently, the military, out of medical necessity, had yanked out all his bad teeth, because of the maintenance issues and had given him the dentures in replacement. He had undergone some kind of physical and psychological transformation. My memories of him are incomplete, after this. I always wondered what his domestic homecoming after the war was like. By documenting these relative events, the legend of the GRMT will live in perpetuity. This, as my fellow comrades and I sought to take a bite out of grime, those many years ago. However, the resolution of a still perplexing and prima facia mystery has not been satisfied. We would like to know, possibly from some master of the universe, "Who…The…Hell…Took…That…Picture"?

The Persian Flaw

The carpet masters of what was ancient Persia have been wonderfully skilled at their craft for centuries. Their products, carpets, are held to be of perfect artistic and physical quality. These are said, after all, to be an extension of the individual makers. For the indigenous buyer, it is a tangible, non-perishable, decorative necessity: to be carefully tread upon. The acquired skill is handed down from generation to generation. To the carpet masters and believers, no one and nothing is perfect, except Allah. Therefore, each carpet had a hidden flaw, purposely woven into it and known only by its maker, as not to usurp the perfection of God. Each of us, as individuals or groups has this hidden "Persian Flaw". In essence, there are imperfections or characteristics that may be unseen to the world, but to each of us is well known.

For a young man, that part of the journey from adolescence to adulthood is at best, difficult. Physical growth is sometimes not accommodated with equally balanced, psychological maturity. Life experience can sometimes be a cruel teacher and taskmaster. The tuition may at times seem high, but if lessons are learned, it may well be worth the cost. I had at times encountered the countenance of the grim reaper and had lived to talk about it. Along with my youth, this left me with a cavalier attitude and feeling of imperviousness. Since the start of my second tour at Bien Hoa, I had made some very good Vietnamese friends. I believe that in the heat of battle, we would have fought and died together. One such friend, although limited in financial resources, had offered to do the town with me. We westerners and Americans had our places and the Vietnamese had theirs. Since I was the one that wanted to know, see and experience everything, I let the potential taste of a new adventure get the best of me and agreed to go into the unknown.

Some of the mannerisms that I tried to adopt and emulate from this foreign culture would not be accepted back home. For instance, in this male dominated culture, if a man sitting next to you liked you, he could place his hand on your leg. Young people of the same gender, who are good friends, sometimes walked holding hands. Public urination and relieving of oneself were open practice. The head of the household might stay out all night, spending the milk money on nefarious episodes of self-indulgence. Those of this persuasion were usually unencumbered by any domestic stigmas. Also, the head of household may have been a vacuous character, but his position was usually unquestioned.

In an associated analogy, bamboo has a natural ability to twist, bend and deform during powerful storms. However, this resiliency allows it to eventually come back together after these periodic storms. Likewise, the natural, indigenous families also came back together after these personal tempests. However difficult or superficial, harmony at home is paramount and Confucian.

I dedicated an afternoon and evening, after work, with the next day off, to recuperate from what I anticipated would be an entirely new experience. First of all, the city of Bien Hoa was off limits to most, American military personnel. There was a risk of being caught by U.S. army military police patrols and the ramifications would be unpleasant. As we left the Vietnamese gate, my friend grasped my hand. It was awkward and my gut feeling was to release his hand. However, I felt that he might be slighted, so I swallowed hard and didn't. We hit a few, local, Vietnamese establishments and the typical patronage was always very similar. Since the pay of the locals was miniscule, compared to ours, the cost of alcohol and bar flies were commensurate. Upon entrance, many of them looked at me with positive astonishment. One place, there was an Asian, beaded alcove, with a very intoxicated man and one of the ladies, "working". When he saw me, he started smiling glassy eyed and began haphazardly waving a black revolver around. He assured me in broken English, that I was covered. Once the patrons got over the initial shock of my extraordinary presence, they appeared to be both honored and delighted, by my attendance. We visited several places, and it was the same scenario. As we ventured, I breathed in and consumed these experiences. They will be encrypted into my memory for posterity and until I am no longer able to remember them. We walked through several meandering warrens. There were tiny alleyways where naked children, as was customary, were playing. To the best of my recollection, we even walked into people's homes, unannounced, uninvited and uninhibited. It was a real rush.

Three of the main elements of any culture are its indigenous languages, religion and its ethnic foods. The Vietnamese culture fell into this context. Originating from China, the nomadic and warlike inhabitants wandered to and settled the Sout East Asia coast. Here, they were to form the nucleus for modern day Vietnam. Their cuisine consisted mainly of offshoot Chinese dishes. It is now influenced by French and sprinkled with a smattering of American accommodations. Vietnamese are very industrious people. Most businesses are small and family run, with numerous mom and pop establishments.

With the sun having slipped below the horizon for awhile now and our stomachs growling, we went to a hole in the wall, "fast food" establishment. These were most common at and concentrated in high traffic areas, of cities. With the look of delight that I was getting from the proprietors, I was sure that I had been among one of the few or even their very first western customers. Our meal was served quickly. It was a native soup. The soup base was chicken broth with tasty meat and vegetables. Except for the crunchy bean sprouts, the spices were unknown to me. However, they made this soup extremely delicious. I can understand why Europeans came to the orient long ago. They risked their lives and fortunes, making perilous journeys to obtain such spices, to flavor their otherwise bland and mundane dishes.

A U.S. army military police patrol happened to pass by, but they did not see me. My friend and the proprietors had some concerns. Bien Hoa had not always been off limits. Americans used to roam the streets and establishments of the city freely. Subsequently, the wild and sometimes outrageous behavior of uninhibited young men, was just too much for the citizenry. With a consensus of opinions, the mayor banned all but essential allied troops and put the city off limits. U.S. troops could always venture down the road to Saigon and realize their needs there. Although there were businesses which catered to Americans that were flourishing, it had been a wise decision.

Going all around town that evening and early morning, I stuck out like a sore thumb, but this was an epic "hang loose" escapade and whatever was going to happen would happen. In town, there was the unmistakable sound of the Lambretta. These were three wheeled taxis that were little more than a jazzed-up motorcycle, which had a roof and held mostly seated passengers. These were also sometimes covered and used for other commercial businesses.

It never ceased to amaze me how these people took every opportunity to hustle a buck. Having hustled for pennies, as a child, there was a shared empathy and understanding for them and penury.

All the optics, sounds and odors of a foreign place were taken in. Now pondering, I couldn't help but wonder what was on the back end of this wild night. It was possible that this escapade could have ended badly, even possibly with my own demise.

Back home in South Carolina, there was a nice cemetery by the tranquil Ashley River, near Charleston. It had some beautiful old oak trees, and the grounds contained the remains of a few relatives already. There would have been a formal military honor guard to give me a traditional gun salute, as my nice new casket was lowered. I wondered who might be getting that new and neatly, triangular folded, American flag? Knowing the nature of my atypical family, there might have been a melodramatic scene. It probably would have been very entertaining. The gang would all be there, familial friends and foes. I could even imagine an appropriate epitaph. "Here lies a brother in arms… he went looking for obvious charms. It was such a youthful blunder…Now, he is six feet under".

We inevitably made it safely to a nice establishment. It was much classier than all the others that we had visited earlier. I was welcomed and put at ease. This place was the icing on the cake. We had a very memorable time. I don't know how much all this adventure cost my friend, but I am confident that it wasn't cheap. It is possible that he had spent what little money he had saved up, over a considerable period. However, he benefitted from a VNAF barracks to stay in, and another pay period that was coming up. As a foreigner, to be given this kind of treatment was nearly unheard of. I conveyed my utmost appreciation to him for his kindness and consideration. We both made it back tired and without any negative consequences from this ebullient and youthful adventure. All was well.

The Drug Bust

As I have previously alluded to, there were two specific gates for Bien Hoa city. Gate one was primary for VNAF and associated personnel. Gate two was primarily, American ingress and egress. Because of the volume of traffic, it was manned by two VNAF and two USAF policemen. That day, I was at gate two. I had noticed the same four army grunts coming through this gate, on several occasions. They were a motley looking bunch, even for field grunt standards. I became suspicious, when the frequency of these entrances had increased. Why weren't they going to the army base through the army gate? What were they doing in the city and why did they have a look of relief on their faces, every time that they were waved through? As my discomfort level and suspicions rose, I watched as they again approached our gate, for entrance. As a self-trained observer, I could read the tenseness and anxiety on their faces. I knew in my guts that something was not as it should be. This time, instead of waving them through, like they had expected, I stopped their jeep. As I approached the driver of the canvas roofed vehicle, I could see that something was amiss, in the faces of the driver and his three passengers. Sensing danger, I visibly unsnapped my service revolver. Mechanically, I told the driver that he, his passengers and their vehicle were going to get a routine shakedown inspection. At this point, they all appeared to be in a state of heightened anxiety. I ordered the driver to move the vehicle over to the side, to ensure a continuous flow of incoming, vehicular traffic. As the jeep eased forward, I noticed that it wasn't stopping and was slowly creeping away. At this point, I was absolutely sure that something was definitely wrong. I raised my pistol and ran to the ever slowly, moving jeep. The driver was ordered to stop immediately. Now, there was an adrenalin rush, as I knew something very big was about to go down. The hairs on the back of my neck were standing up and my heart was pounding. I called a colleague over to cover me and to add more security and firepower. I had him audibly chamber a round on his M-16. Subsequently, I recalled a previous conversation that I had with an army policeman. He related to me that illegal drugs were sometimes hidden in the engine compartment. So, I walked up to the front of the jeep, unlatched the hood and tilted it back against the windshield. As I scanned through the engine compartment, I noticed that there was a green colored, cloth laundry bag. This bag was pulled out and placed on top of the now closed hood. The occupants in the front seats now had a "scared rabbit" look on their faces. As I unraveled the bag, I could see a large, rectangular package, wrapped in brown paper and tied neatly with twine. My heart raced and my hands trembled as I opened the package. Even after previous situations that I had been in as a law enforcement specialist, I was excited. Finally, the package was opened, and its contents exposed. There in front of me were ultimately, a large number of vials, containing nearly pure heroin. I ordered the occupants out of the jeep and told them i.e. that one wrong move and someone was going to get shot! It was that serious and a point had to be made.

This whole episode was very surreal and now, almost overwhelming. Before this tense situation went any further, I got on the radio and called for immediate reinforcement and transportation of the suspects. While we waited, time seemed to be static. I also remembered from my previous discussions, with other military policemen that contraband was also sometimes hidden, in a compartment, near the front right passenger's seat. I went over and folded the seat forward and lifted it up to check this space; there appeared to be a couple of green, military sandbags. These "sandbags" were pulled out and upon examination, they were found to be full of packed marijuana. This was a second strike and I then realized that these individuals were major drug mules and dealers. The wait for assistance was lengthy. Just before help arrived, I noticed that some of them probably had packages of cigarettes in their chest pockets. In a few of my previous minor drug busts, I found that individuals were buying mentholated cigarettes and were manually removing the tobacco. This was then carefully replaced with packed marijuana. So, whenever they wanted to get high, it would be mentholated, drawn evacuation. The tops of each of these packages that I removed appeared to be unopened. However, when they were turned upside down, I could see that each of them had small tears, on the bottoms. Sure enough, each package contained marijuana, as well. A visual clue was the twisted ends. I had just scored a once in a lifetime drug bust trifecta. Finally, I was made aware that the flight chief was on his way, and wood soon be there.

One of the now very nervous suspects made a surprise inquiry. "Hey man, I want to know my rights?" In all the quickly unfolding drama, I had forgotten to read them all their rights, under the UCMJ. I am not sure if this oversight could have been used as a future point of contention. However, I responded with an acknowledgement of the oversight and thanked the individual for reminding me. This was not received well (burn) and then I proceeded to inform them of their rights. Upon completion of this, the flight chief belatedly arrived. I advised the chief of what had transpired, including the large amount of heroin and marijuana. Astonished, he distinctly uttered an expletive. Now, he was beside himself. Because of the large group of suspects, another patrol had to be called in to help with transportation.

I rode in with the team back to security control. The individuals were placed in confinement and were held for transportation by U.S. army authorities, back to be processed. I waited to be on hand for any further questions, still immersed in this surreal moment. One thing that I do remember, is that there was no immediate "pat on the back" from our office supervision. Of course, they would all find some way to attach themselves to "their win" as they always seemed to do. Although this was a given, it was still unprofessional and a typical slight. What happened the rest of that day, is just a complete blur now.

A few days later, I along with the other policeman that was a backup for this drug bust was called to the base commanders' office. The colonel asked me to give him a detailed, verbal account on what had taken place, as he had a great interest in it. This briefing was very well received, and he personally thanked me for a job well done. Furthermore, he stated that at the very minimum I would receive a tangible memento of appreciation. This would initially be an inscribed plaque. In addition, there would quite possibly be a meritorious bronze star medal. I would later be informed that mine was the biggest drug bust in the history of that installation. After meeting with the colonel, I was euphoric. The personal thank you from our base commander was the best salve for the recent, in-house slight. However, this story would later take a bizarre and dangerous turn.

I was eventually summoned to go to the 1st Air Cavalry legal office and gave a lengthy statement, to an army lawyer. These soldiers had been caught red handed, trafficking assorted drugs. It was now in the hands of army investigators and the legal process had been initiated. Although I am not privy to the ultimate outcome of the cases, each one of them had basically ruined their young lives and future. Probably, there would be some incarcerations and bad conduct discharges. There was not one minute of lost sleep, on my part. Whether by greed or addiction, they had created their own nightmare and a merciless example had to be made of them. This event was just a microcosm of the associated drug problems, during the war.

Some period of time would go by, before I was informed that I was going to be officially presented with a plaque, at a ceremony, in the base theater. The official presentation was going to be from the base commander to me and this was quite an honor. A time and date were determined, and I was informed of this. On the day of the presentation, I was atypically assigned to a rare posting at the far end of the base, which abutted some local village and rice field. Finding this odd, I reminded the supervisor, who posted me that I had an important ceremony that day, with the base commander and that I didn't want to miss it. I was assured that all was well. However, as the hour approached, no one had come. Unfortunately, because of the distance and location, the radio communication was sometimes intermittent. Finally, I could hear and then see a jeep on a tear, coming to me. The driver was a staff sergeant lifer, that I was aware of being involved in corrupt dealings. There was no reason given for this tardy pick up, as we sped to the/my ceremony. When we got to the theater, people were already leaving. I was then approached by an admonishing supervisor, who asked me why I did not make it in time for the important presentation. I told him that I had just been relieved and delivered there.

We just looked at each other momentarily and no more words were spoken. My moment of focused praise and military glory had been taken from me and I was certain that it was no accident. It was an acute, psychological gut punch. Too many things just did not add up. Along with this, the meritorious bronze star did not materialize, as well. I believe that illegal drug commerce had some high reaching tentacles. And as things played out, this retaliation was not just not paranoia. There would later be a near fatal incident, which I absolutely believe was related.

However, I was eventually called into our squadron commanders office, where I was finally and belatedly thanked for my effort and presented with the aforementioned plaque. I was also given a copy of black and white photographs of the heroin vials and "sandbags" of marijuana, spread neatly, across a table. Suspiciously, I found it to be very strange that the packages of marijuana cigarettes were not there.

I also have the photograph of our squadron commander, presenting me with this nice plaque. This was appreciatively received, although with a diminished sense of satisfaction. I still have this plaque and display it proudly.It reads:

SECURITY MAN OF THE MONTH

JUNE 1971

PRESENTED TO

SGT. MICHAEL R. FARLEY

6251 SECURITY POLICE SQUADRON

The Cobra

In Vietnam, during the war, there were two types of cobras. One was a heavily armed platform, built into a military helicopter. The other kind of cobra was a species of deadly, poisonous snakes. Because of numerous mongoose sightings on the base, we let these predators roam free, to take care of the snake population. As I have stated, the military complex at Bien Hoa was sprawling. The connecting army base was the domicile of the 1st Air Cavalry. The only joint gate between the USAF/VNAF was what we called the "Army Gate". It was manned jointly by a USA military policeman and a USAF security policeman. Sometimes, there was a VNAF QC (military policeman).

One day, I was on patrol as a team leader of a joint allied security patrol, which covered the air base. This gun crew consisted of a seasoned Air Force NCO and two Vietnamese counterparts. We got a call from control (CSC) that the security policeman at the army gate needed a 10-14 or latrine break. When we pulled up to the gate, I saw that it was another sergeant that lived in my barracks. The closest facility was a considerable distance away. He told me that it was urgent, so he decided to just go into a nearby, prepositioned Conex box. These were supposed to be used as an alternate cover from the periodic rocket attacks. They were small, box/ rectangle shaped steel structures, with one side hinged open, to enter and exit. This particular gate was on a small hill, up and away from the base proper. At this isolated position, we could hear the enemy launched rockets approaching, before they hit the occupied base area. The best audio of these missiles was during the hours of darkness and when humidity was high. The sound was analogous to a low flying jet. I can remember at least one occasion at this location, screaming "incoming!". The USAF call sign for this was 10-88 and it was the very last thing that you wanted to hear come across the radio. The nighttime optics of these explosive impacts were terrifying. There was a bright orange flash and then a mushroom fireball, which rolled upward. The deadly components were the blast and the jagged shrapnel.

With some foresight, at least one roll of toilet paper was kept at this gate. The sergeant grabbed the paper and quickly disappeared into the Conex. Shortly thereafter, we heard screams; "snake! snake!" and at least one gunshot immediately rang out. The next thing that we all saw was this sergeant running out, holding his lowered trousers in one hand and his pistol in the other hand. He had a terrified look on his face. This rocket shelter was dimly illuminated, with ambient light. There was now an immediate concern that this snake was poisonous and that it could emerge and possibly harm one of us. I then quickly got out with my wooden truncheon in hand and approached the entrance. As I stepped inside and my eyes adjusted, I observed ground movement, in the back, left corner. Because of the close quarters and possible ricochet, I did not fire at it. Therefore, I rushed over to it and beat it with my truncheon, until there was no more movement. When I felt that it was safe, I picked up the snake by its tail and slowly backed out into the sunlight. When my Vietnamese counterparts saw this huge snake, there became very excited and animated. One of them pointed to the snakes' head and as I got a closer look at it, my heart almost stopped. It then became very clear that I had just had a very close encounter with and was now holding, one of the deadliest snakes in the world. It was a cobra. As we were talking, a couple of army grunts pulled up to the gate, to enter the air base. I walked over with the snake to the gate, showed it to them and told them it was a cobra. I remember the skeptical driver telling me that I was wrong. However, as I then pulled the skin on its head out to expose the classic cobra hooded head, he sat in stunned silence. Yes… it was a cobra! It is interesting that the requesting sergeant now no longer needed a latrine break. After he calmed down and resumed his duties, we left. In retrospect, what started out as a mundane task could have easily become a tragedy. The relieved sergeant or I could have been bitten, by this deadly serpent and then quickly become a non-combat, casualty death.

Prior to each working shift, we had our regular briefing. This was to go over assignments, hot topics, listen to the latest inane, job justification memorandums from back office, "desk jockeys" and check weapons. Once we broke for our fixed posts or patrols, we were more or less without much support. Although we had shift supervisors, they usually went back to the control office. Here was a nice, comfortable air-conditioned building, away from the bugs, elements and malfeasants that we had to deal with on a daily basis. This structure also housed our squadron management hierarchy and brass.

We were out in the intense heat and sometimes drenching rain showers, while trying to execute law enforcement and security jobs. These were tasks that brought us little praise, some scorn and much hardship. There was a common joke that we and the back office worked on a fifty- fifty basis. We did most of the dirty work and they got most of the credit.

At this juncture, a timely epiphany had presented itself. I then placed the dead snake in an empty sandbag and headed back to CSC. Once parked, I grabbed the bag, walked back to the heart of operations, then stopped and looked at them. They all stopped what they were doing and looked at me. I remember asking the group if any of them had ever seen a cobra. I then removed the snake from the bag; grabbed its head, spread its hood and held it up so that they all could see that it was a real cobra. There were now stunned looks and gasps of astonishment. Some even moved their wheeled chairs back, in obvious trepidation. I just wanted to let them know, by presentation, that this was an example of what we on the line had to deal with, on a daily basis. Given their immediate reaction, the point was apparently well proven.

I placed the snake securely in the bag and got back into my patrol unit. One of my Vietnamese colleagues told me that he would like to have it to eat, so I gave it to him, and he was a very happy camper! When I eventually got off from work that day, the base seemed to be buzzing about an "outlandish rumor". It appears that some audacious Air Force cop had personally taken out a deadly cobra in close quarters. He then brought in the proof, to make a point to the back office. I was relieved when the notoriety had finally worn off. It seems that most had to listen to the story from beginning to end, over and over again. For me, it had just been another day at work. However, amongst our finite community and contemporaries, this saga was now legend.

Serpents

The natural world is out and open, filled with many beasts.

Some work hard, some do not, they take up space, at least.

Deeds and words are who we are, in places near and far.

Sometimes we wonder which is worse, given all the stakes.

A slithering reptile on the ground or walking human snakes.

Bodyguard

We were all excited that the entourage of Bob Hope's last USO show would initially arrive at Bien Hoa AB. The word soon got out that these VIPs would need bodyguards, for their brief appearance at our base. A handful of us felt very lucky to be selected for this potentially dangerous, yet, once in a lifetime experience. We were briefed by our commander. The captain told us that we were to use our bodies as human shields and to protect these "high value resources" at all costs. At the time, these solemn orders had little impact on us. The excitement of the event provided us with a sense of elated anticipation. We were given a heads up, just before the aircraft, with its precious cargo arrived. There was a large crowd forming, at the edge of the flight line. This group contained a mix of mostly military personnel and some civilians. We were charged to tune out the celebrities and be extremely vigilant for any potential life-threatening scenarios. These were especially and specifically, hidden threats or bad actors, which may have blended into the crowd.

The military cargo aircraft, with its nose and fore section painted red and white, taxied in. As the propellers slowed to a stop, we moved into place. Our shield initially formed, at the aft cargo ramp, which began lowering, until grounded. Among the first to deplane was Bob Hope himself. I can't speak for the others, but this was one of the most gratifying moments of my Vietnam experience. His friendly "blue collar" greetings brought the security contingency back down to earth.

He had looked at his security detail momentarily and we all saw a warm, genuine human being. He was a popular, world class superstar, but he was also a regular guy. These USO shows were potentially dangerous, yet he gave of himself freely. We would have put ourselves on the line for this man and this group, if we had to, with no qualms.

As we shook ourselves back to reality, other celebrities came down the ramp. Baseball great Johnny Bench, along with some beautiful women, presented themselves. We were informed that one of these ladies was the reigning Miss World. Her effervescence was contagious, her youthful beauty breathtaking and extraordinary. All of us there, probably would have easily voted her, Miss "Out of This World!" She wore a camouflaged, cowboy hat and a wonderfully short, open knitted, mini skirt. Of course, I was fortunate enough to be able to take a quick picture of her and Bob Hope.

Superstar Bob Hope walked up to the placed microphone, as if it were second nature. He had on a red baseball cap and carried a gulf club, as a prop. He kept the packed crowd enthralled and at ease, with a series of jokes and anecdotes. It was a real challenge to watch for potential threats, control the crowd, cover the celebrities and take a few quick photos, but I did. I was not going to let this once in a lifetime opportunity pass, without photographic documentation, for posterity. We tried our best to push the overwhelming crowd back, without much success. Even if there was a bad actor, he or she probably would have been prevented from their assignment, by a "body wall". All but one in this prestigious group appeared open, approachable and friendly. Without exposing the name, this individual was at least there, giving up personal time and taking a risk. Finally, the group, in its entirety, boarded a military bus and left for its next destination. They would do their skits and strut their stuff, on that last USO show.

I was a bodyguard, on one other occasion. Another star was coming. It was Sammy Davis Jr. and I remember it well. His plane arrived and taxied some distance from a very large crowd of servicemen. It was extremely hot. However, the diminishing prop wash of the engines gave us some momentary relief, until they came to a full stop. The associated fumes also permeated the air. Again, our detail waited and watched as the ramp door descended to the ground. After all the times I had seen this gifted actor on TV, I wasn't quite sure what to expect. He slowly emerged and I was somewhat taken aback. Standing in front of me was a short, diminutive man, that could have easily been drawn as a children's stick figure. However, his casual smile helped assuage us all. I then wondered how so much gifted talent could come from this little man?

We secured him and went directly to the awaiting crowd of admirers. His entourage left after a short period of "rapping, dapping and tapping". My experiences as a bodyguard were brief, but memorable. I can readily identify and empathize with those that do it on a daily, professional basis. They earn every penny that they make, and it is a job that I would not likely have done for a living.

An Orchid in The Minefield

It was the spring of 1972, at Bien Hoa AB, Republic of Vietnam and toward the end of my third and final tour of duty. President Nixon's plan to extricate America from this conflict had been implemented. It was promoted as "Peace with Honor" and it had been negotiated by secretary of state Henry Kissinger, at the Paris peace conference. American and other allied soldiers were being replaced by our Vietnamese counterparts, in a process called "Vietnamization". In essence, America was weary of this far away, unpopular war and the accumulative costs of our blood and treasure. This was the plausible, face-saving vehicle used to cut our losses and come home. Being a senior, law enforcement patrolman, on day shift had its perks. Recognition of experience by your peers was one of the few intangible credits given.

According to the politics of the time, all of the U.S. marines had been officially withdrawn from the country. This was the official version. In reality, not only had they not been withdrawn, but I was also working with them. There was a marine jet fighter unit that was somewhat covertly flying missions out of Bien Hoa AB. They had their own maintenance crews and their own separate barracks, which housed them. I had to respond to a few law enforcement calls to these barracks and also pulled security with them, as the team leader. One of the interesting jobs in my position was meeting VIP's and American news reporters of the day. I got a call to report to a public relations officer, one day. I was to be given the task as a "minder" for NBC news reporter, Arthur Lord and his film crew. My instructions were to escort them to various locations, but to avoid taking them to any location that the marines might be at. I met Mr. Lord and he seemed to be a down to earth guy. He asked to be escorted to the bomb dump and I complied. The crew filmed a story about the ammunition being used. When this was finished, I escorted them back out, so they could check with the public relations office. While we were waiting for the PR officer, I had a casual conversation with Mr. Lord. He half-jokingly asked me to take him to the marines "That aren't here". We both knew how the game was being played. As the PR officer showed up, I told him that I was there with my brother and that this was my third and last tour. The PR officer suggested that he do a story on this. However, he declined. After I returned back home, I watched some of Arthur Lord's reports on TV.

It wasn't long after this that I found myself, alone on patrol. As the most senior, first term patrol NCO, I had virtually cart blanche of the whole, expansive installation. My stint in the war would be ending soon and this solitary duty gave me time for philosophical reflection. This entire experience had left an indelible impression on me. The blazing sun, with the associated heat and the humidity was nearly insufferable. The number of troops that were coming in was fewer and fewer. I had at times been disillusioned by the many wrongs that were observed and experienced. I believed that America was being played and used by a very corrupt government. The ARVN or Army of the Republic of Vietnam, were mostly, inept cannon fodder. They had some professionals and a few good units, but not many. It was quite obvious to me and others how this all would turn out, once we left. I remember commenting that this allied installation would transition into a communist base, with MIG aircraft, in ten years. This statement proved to be prophetic and actual.

I drove my jeep past the army gate, then to our back and parallel to the runways. This area was hilly and desolate. As I drove, I was deep in thought. However, on one of the hills, overlooking a runway, I just happened to momentarily spot a very beautiful flower, in a field. In retrospect, I believe that this was a wild orchid. It seemed very odd that something as beautiful as this had not been removed by the locals, as they had a propensity to "secure" anything of beauty and value that was not nailed down and guarded. I was mesmerized by this emblem of beauty, surrounded by all the ugliness of war. As I sat in my jeep, I was in awe and admiration of such a rare entity. It was there that all inhibitions of defense mechanisms were vacated. The only thing I wanted to do in this moment was touch this tangible beauty and venerate it, close up.

Just outside the single strand of barbed wire, I got out of my jeep. I removed my blue, security police helmet and my web belt with my pistol and sheathed bayonet. I laid my radio and only means of communication in the front passenger seat. I now only had one purpose in life and that was to go to that alluring orchid. I remember stepping over the single strand of barbed wire and steadily approaching my goal. As I walked towards it, I just happened to step by a large, cracked opening in the dried, clay earth. This clay soil would be saturated by the tropical rain and then crack open, as it was quickly dried by the sun. To my utmost horror, I could see a landmine in the cracked earth. As I immediately came to my senses, I realized that this beautiful flower was untouched for a reason. It was at the far end of the minefield, and I was standing at the geometric center of a man made, killing field. Looking over to the single stranded barbed wire, I could now clearly see the red triangular signs, with the skull and cross bones. I had let my guard down, having been lured by this fleur fatale.

Although it was intensely hot, my body felt completely ice cold. These mine fields had been laid out by experts, to ensure that anyone entering would probably not survive. My thoughts were, "I am going to die!". My only means of communication was in my jeep, along with a .38 pistol that I could have fired to get someone's attention. With no head covering, the potential for heat stroke and unconsciousness were pronounced. I wondered how painful an exploding mine would be and what would the death experience be like. The reusable military coffins were cleaned ready to go for the next candidate. Where would I be buried and who would come? The grim reaper was at hand.

Traumatized, I digressed back to when I was a child and member of the First Baptist Church of Hialeah (Florida). Things were so simple back then. We were impressed to be innocent and believe in a higher power. Then back to reality, the words came. "Yea though I walk through the valley of the shadow of death, I will fear no evil". There was a calmness. I checked the ground to see my footsteps, after entering. They were barely visible, but they were there. Pivoting, I placed one foot onto a previous place of ground, recently disturbed by my incoming footsteps. There was no explosion. I gingerly repeated this method, until there was only a couple of steps left, but no visually disturbed ground. Building confidence that I was going to beat this, I started to put a foot down, but stopped as my foot was almost on the ground. A mental warning sounded. As I turned my foot slightly, I could see the plunger of a land mine that I was about to step on. I put my foot down, adjacent to it. One more step to go and over the wire to safety. I stepped over and I was out. All this time,

I could hear the radio squawking. Someone was trying to contact me. Not wasting any time, I got back into the jeep, turned over the ignition, placed it into gear and put as much distance between me and the minefield as I expeditiously could. Now, who was ever going to believe this extraordinary story and who would I even tell? I raced back to the control center and front desk. Someone there said, "Where the hell were you? We have been trying to get you on the radio!" I remember responding, "I have been busy trying to walk out of a minefield!" They all laughed. So, did I.

Although my combat duty there at Bien Hoa AB was winding down, there would be yet one more close encounter with the hereafter, and I would leave that encounter still standing also. It was a phase in my young adult life, in which I was giving any cat with nine lives, a real run for its money.

Sleeping Soldiers

It was 1972 and my last tour of duty, in the Republic of Vietnam. As a military policeman, enforcing and adjudicating the Uniform Code of Military Justice (UCMJ) was a very difficult occupation, especially in a combat zone. Although it applied to all, getting the message out was equally difficult. The commissioned officers were much more adherent to the rules, but at times, had to be handled with kid gloves. The vast majority of our problems came from the lower enlisted ranks. Just going to work to do our jobs was stressful and we all looked forward to our off time. The various avenues of decompression were tied overwhelmingly to personal funds on hand. Our monthly paydays were a much-anticipated event. The U.S. government provided us with the necessary food, shelter and clothing required. Paydays were the icing on the cake, especially for those of us that were not married and had few financial commitments.

After payday, there was a general and collective jovial mood. The clubs would fill, alcohol would be consumed in large quantities and the various illegal drugs for those that did this, would be acquired for immediate consumption. At this time, it was not very difficult to catch a distinguishable whiff of disbursed marijuana smoke, in the evenings or early mornings. The sometimes audible, female laughter of "ladies", behind closed doors was periodic. They always knew when we got paid. This was one of the two times a month that policing services were usually required the most. The other period that we were busy was in between paydays. As the days went by after being paid, the mood usually digressed and that is when calls for USAF cops were again elevated. Young men with preeminent hormone levels, confined together in this dangerous atmosphere and little money, sometimes had short fuses.

Our base at Bien Hoa was about an hour away by car, from Saigon, the capital of South Vietnam. The direct route to there was via Highway One. However, to get leave to go to Saigon required written permission, but for us, that was not usually a problem. Sometimes the commander did not sign a pass or was unavailable to do so. For this specific reason, we had tactically "procured" a special supply of them. A select few of us took turns annotating the commander's signature, with considerable robust and jocular pleasure. The next task, after this, was to go to the city gate and catch a ride. This particular morning, I was easily able to get a ride, going to Saigon. We mechanically weaved our way, from the busy streets in the city of Bien Hoa and then onto Highway One, for the routine trip. It was a nice day and there was the usual bustle and mass of humanity. However, when we had gotten a considerable distance down the road, there seemed to be a lot of civilian, police activity. As we crept forward, I could see what appeared to be the epicenter of flashing lights and frantic people. In the distance was a very large military troop carrier that was lying on its side. When we got right up to it, I could see that it was a Thai, military vehicle. On the ground next to it was a field full of mostly prone soldiers, in new, green uniforms. All of these were covered up or were being covered. They were all dead and their bodies were now soulless vessels. This had either been the result of an enemy action or a terrible vehicle accident. The scene was shocking, horrendous and surreal. I could eventually make out some of the faces of these young, Thai soldiers. Some were contorted and others were on their backs. After the initial shock, I felt a sense of personal heartbreak, for their individual families back home. These were the husbands, brothers and sons that they would never hold, share collective laughter or plan a future together, with again. Their loved ones would be notified very soon, and their individual, familial world would be absolutely shattered by the tragic news.

We eventually made it past this scene of palpable horror and went into the heart of Saigon. This trip was just another one, to blow off steam, consume spirits and just have a good time, in general. However, on this occasion, things were completely different. Furthermore, we were all in a combat zone, where lives were constantly imperiled and extinguished; things were irrevocably broken. The reality of this situation had hardened all of us, to a certain degree. Nevertheless, I just could not get the terrible scenes of those lost soldiers out of my thoughts. Subsequently, all of us are imbued with a natural ability to cope with forlorn experiences. This is by way of rationalization. Even now at times, I can still see these forever, young men that did their duty and died too soon. Nevertheless, they are all at peace now for an eternity. These were allied comrades in arms that have rightfully earned this tranquility and apotheosis. Rest well, sleeping soldiers.

The Cherry Bar Run

It was April of 1972, and the war was winding down for American combat forces. In the following year, a peace accord would be signed in Paris and the last official combat soldiers would leave. The country of South Vietnam would have to fend for itself, and extrication of allied troops had already begun. North Vietnam was eagerly anticipating signing this peace agreement; of which it had absolutely no intention of abiding by. The reality was that living in RVN for years, I would be going home soon. My one hundred day "short calendar" was now showing obvious signs of maturity. Additionally, since the capital of Saigon was becoming more and more dangerous, fewer of us were going there, for safety reasons. There were, however, a small cadre of daring or cavalier personalities that did venture out, into the adjoining city of Bien Hoa. Fitting into that later category, it was just a matter of when, not if, I would be going in for another visit.

My friend JK and I had gone to the NCO club to get our minds off the war. There was a good Filipino band and a couple of pretty "go-go" girl dancers. We were there for some period, when we concluded that it was probably time to make a run into town. My brother was working as a customs inspector, assigned to an army unit and lived in a different barracks. We stopped by and woke him, and he was then appraised of our nocturnal plans. He shook himself awake, got dressed, grabbed the pistol that was under his pillow and tagged along. On the way out, I got the pistol that was under my pillow, as well. We all caught a ride to the city gate, manned by VNAF police. Since we worked with them, they knew us well. Because the enemy had been coming in closer and appeared bolder, the base was under "condition yellow". This meant that there was a possibility of an enemy attack. Our friends, at the gate warned us to be careful and let us pass.

We soon arrived at the "Cherry Bar" a local hot spot. It was patronized by allied troops, and it wasn't our first time there.

As we got seated, the opportunistic bar flies vied for attention. The compulsory "Saigon Tea" was ordered for the girls and the superficial chit chat began. There were a few uniformed Korean soldiers in the place and that made us a little uneasy. Things got a little tense when one of them that was obviously intoxicated, walked over to our table. In perfect English, he asked, “Hey man, you got a light”? Subsequently, the cigarette that was dangling from his mouth was amicably lit. The tension only subsided when he went back to his group.

It was already late at night and all of us were tired. The slow moving, overhead fans just moved the hot air around and helped blow the merciless mosquitoes off course. The proprietress was eventually summoned to secure rooms, which were above the business area. Although the rooms were quite small, the beds were comfortable. Sometime afterwords, and now covered in perspiration, a shower was requested. A towel was supplied, and I was led outside, through a back door. A very dim light illuminated a bare bone, makeshift shower. There was no choice of hot or cold, it was just ambient temperature. I was enjoying the mesmerizing view of a very feminine silhouette, when my brother came barreling past yelling “MP, MP”! He and his companion had gone up front to a soup joint, to work out on some delicious, noodle soup or Pho. This is a ubiquitous national dish, and it is consumed at all hours. Apparently, a U.S army jeep patrol had spotted him, as they drove past. One of them yelled “Hey you”! The only option was to run back and warn us. I raced back to my room, put on some underclothes, kicked the rest of my garments under my bed and grabbed my pistol. I could hear momma san arguing downstairs in Vietnamese, with the local “white mice” (civilian police). “Americans, what Americans”? Of course, this was a well-rehearsed ploy, to give us some time to be hidden. Any unauthorized American caught on the premises, after curfew, would probably mean a fine or larger bribe to the authorities.

The establishment would suffer, and this was not an acceptable option. An individual guided me down the stairs to a security door, which was unlocked and opened. My friend JK was already there. Clearly, this was an in place, contingency plan.

Next, we both were led around a corner. A door was opened, and we then went inside a dwelling and into a room. It appeared to be some kind of familial root or dry food, storage area. On the other side of the room, was an open window, to a home. Herein, a black and white TV was playing some kind of Vietnamese soap opera. Within close proximity to us, a white-haired old man was asleep, in a mosquito netted hammock and snoring. Our presence was not acknowledged and was in fact ignored. Apparently, we had not been their first, after hour “guests”. We waited for a while. Someone then came and suggested that we should surrender my brother, as a sacrificial offering, to get the police off of their backs. This was not an acceptable option, and it was therefore declined. As time went by, we made a considerable donation to the indigenous mosquito population. We waited and waited. Finally, the door was opened, and we were led back to the rear entrance of the Cherry Bar. A resident, BT, told me that a white mouse had grilled her when he saw my G.I. boots, under the small bed. Everybody knew the score, but eventually, they did begrudgingly leave. There would be no illicit pay off, on this event. After this excitement, things finally quieted down and we all settled in for the rest of the night. The slow moving, overhead fan on body perspiration had a cooling effect. A very deep sleep came easy and quickly. However, this night was not over yet.

Time passed, then the explosions and concussive waves of the rocket attack impact, rattled the room. Then more rockets slammed onto the air base. Gunfire could be heard, somewhere in the distance. The foreboding attack siren began wailing its frightening tune. Within minutes, we were dressed, in the common hallway and armed. The possibility of our military base being hit was always there. You just learned to take this for granted, once a few of these attacks were under your belt. Standard operating procedure on the base was to take immediate cover and then wait for the "all clear". We then mustered to the armory to get weapons and assignments. I had secured a post attack assignment on a "crater team". It was our job to locate the rocket impacts. When we found the smoking remains, we placed an instrument in it, to locate and find the direction in which it had been fired. This was called in and an appropriate response was weighed. My absence would be noticed.

By virtue of our off-base location, the three of us were now facing an immediate conundrum. If you did not make it to muster, you had better be wounded or you'd have some heavy duty explaining to do. Now, what were we to do? A difficult choice had to be made. We could stay, until we felt that it was safe or try to make it back to the base. The problem with the latter was that leaving immediately could put us face to face with Viet Cong elements. There would be an inevitable shoot out, with the outcome questionable. While we were trying to come to a consensus, momma san appeared and vehemently stated. "You no go, VC come; VC come"! She seemed to be sincerely anguished and that was very disturbing. Beneath her matronly appearance was a street smart, hard and savvy woman. In retrospect, she may have gotten her start as "one of the girls" in her youth, near the end of the French colonial rule. Now, an older, faded beauty, she probably left many a legionnaire, with some very pleasant memories.

As the unquestioned boss of this establishment, her word here was one of keenly acquired knowledge and had to be considered. If she said that Charlie was in the area, then it was gospel. There may have been a supplemental concern. Three dead American servicemen, right outside of her place would be extremely bad for business. This was a country at war and one with few social safety nets. That approaching retirement, to a home in the cool mountains of Dalat, would have to be postponed. Further speculating: the additional payoffs would be considerable. The superficial indignity of condescending, local officials would have to be dealt with. More liberal access to the girls by “pillars of the community” would cut deeper into profits. However, these benefits were just another overhead cost, in the nature of this business.

A decision had to be made and was made. We were young, fit and armed and would therefore, run the unknown gauntlet. If there was to be a confrontation with the enemy, we would just have to possibly shoot it out. If we didn’t make it, there would be some interesting stories in the newspapers and somebody else would have to enlighten and satiate curiosity. If we did make it, a very plausible explanation would be needed, but we would still be alive. We were all presently at the back door and then outside. There was no more pleading from momma san; just the sound of the door being heavily bolted behind us. Now, there was absolutely no going back. Should we make a few blocks before being taken out, her potential problems would dissipate. Of course, there would be the inevitable investigation, with pressure from the U.S. government. Momma san would probably tell officials with a straight face, “They were never here”! A small donation to Budda and the lighting of three scented prayer sticks in the temple, would forever absolve her of any feelings of guilt or remorse.

So, it was now or never and off we went. With weapons drawn, the road back was crisscrossed, a few houses at a time. At different places, we heard splashing sounds, talking and intermittent gunfire.

Every time we ran and stopped; we pressed our backs against each wall; hoping to keep incrementally, lower profiles. At one point, I wanted to be a painting or wall mural. I needed to be anywhere but where we were. How did we get ourselves unnecessarily placed in this predicament? Maybe this was just a bad dream, and I would soon wake up in the relative comfort of my own barracks bed. Few, in this theater of operations could escape, routine bad dreams, i.e. nightmares. However, our latest endeavor had put tangible legs on this one.

We began to hear the unmistakable sound of a Lambretta taxi coming towards our location. Its single, distinct light was off, for some reason. This was possibly a mechanical malfunction or given the circumstances, the individual could have been a bad player. In retrospect, I'll go with the latter. It came out of the darkness, like a surreal apparition. The next thing that JK and in knew, my brother jumped out in front of the taxi and pointed his pistol at the suspicious driver, who then came to a stop. A pistol in hand and body language needs no verbal translation. It was curious that this guy just happened to appear, right after the gunfire had ceased. Maybe he had just dropped off some of his VC buddies, to take out targets of opportunity, like us. We pointed in the direction that we needed to go. The taxi turned around and took off. In front of our main gate was a red and white checkered water tower, for the city of Bien Hoa. The driver stopped when it came into view. We got out and the driver went on his way, with the light still out. I can say with the greatest amount of certainty that the taxi driver was not a very happy character.

Now, we had to make it to the gate, without being killed, by our own colleagues. This would be the next and probably last obstacle to overcome. However, as we slowly approached the back side of the water tower, we came upon a gruesome sight. There, in front of us were two dead people. They had not been dead long, and their blood had streamed. There was this horrific sight and a germane odor, which blended into the humid air. It is not out of the realm of possibility that, having arrived a little earlier, this could have been the three of us lying there. We slipped around those bodies, made it to the water tower and collected ourselves. The main gate was now in front of us and there were some voices that were barely audible at this distance. Dialing in, it was apparent that one of those voices was a lifer. Even if we avoided "friendly fire" this career man could write us up and rat us out. Finally, after a period of time, he left. It was again, now or never, and the decision was made to approach the gate. Making a running dash might have been deadly, so that was out. So, we slowly walked forward, until we were recognized. A familiar and heavily, German accented voice yelled out, "Halt or I shoot; Halt or I shoot"! As fate would have it, this was same guy, once again pointing a weapon at me and threatening to shoot. We yelled out our names to identify ourselves, along with a few choice words. Our very anxious compatriot told us to put our hands up where he could see them and to walk in. We walked to the gate and more words were exchanged. The VNAF gate cops seemed completely enthralled at our incredible audacity. Somehow, we had made it back in one piece and unwounded. We all checked in and were questioned about our tardiness. Of course, this was most assuredly due to all of the confusion, with respect to the enemy attack. There would be no more "Runs" and this was our last one together. The Fates had been teased too many times. I will never forget that night, albeit one of wild and youthful indiscretions.

Youth

The inexperience of one's youth will manifest foolish things.
One mistake, one step too far, may yield a harp and wings.

It is said we come this way but once, no need to make a plan.
To live, to die, one could care less, do all the things you can.

Through the gauntlet of experience, the sand of time does fall.
Come listen, by the hand of fate, you'll hear the final call.

Spring once bourne gives way to summer, and times that
passion enters.
We choose our paths and when it's fall, we hope for many
winters.

Time stands still for no one; this we know too well.
One day we come, one day we go and leave this earthly shell.

Michael R. Farley

Improvised Explosive Device

I was nearing the end of my final tour of duty, in Vietnam. I had initially entered the country as an unworldly teenager, but now and a few years later, there were experiences and memories that had been imbedded for a lifetime. Whatever residue of innocence that I had brought with me, in the beginning, was now spent and gone. While working in the legal field of military law enforcement, there was an exposition of how life actually was. This experience had been a real worldly education and an eye opener. There were some good personal reasons for serving voluntarily, in this theater of conflict. I had embraced another culture and had developed a good working knowledge of another language, as well. Immersing into this different culture satisfactorily, had been a challenge, but I had achieved a suitable level of accomplishment. As a young policeman, we had been given considerable authority, with respect to our uniformed service members. However, being in this position meant that those individuals we had to usually deal with were not the cream of our society. Rather, too many were nonconformists in uniform that had been collected and placed, in this historic crucible of war.

At this time, the American military services made an attempt to vet their recruits. However, it became obvious to me that too many had gotten through, which should have never been in a military uniform. During my service in Vietnam, I had witnessed much wrongdoing and especially corruption, by too many of those in an elevated, position of authority. There were unlawful renumerations for illicit things in cash, sex and other beneficial accommodations. The government of this country that America poured so much of its human resources and treasure into, was thoroughly corrupt. With the exception of some core professionals, its army was incompetent. We all had a fair idea that there would be a collapse and capitulation, after the U.S. withdrew and after the acclaimed Paris Peace

Accords was fully implemented. The North would just wait for American withdrawal, before reneging then invading and conquering the South.

I am aware of at least one protection scheme of an on base civilian entity, which involved mid-level, USAF police. I also personally witnessed a Base Exchange security official punching multiple, empty holes on a military ration card. This was for another law enforcement supervisor and fellow lifer. The perpetrator then loaded up the rationed items in our patrol jeep, with apparent impunity. He then took these "black-market" goods off base to sell them to eagerly awaiting civilians. It was obvious to me that this was a regular routine. It was so open and blatant that it took me completely by surprise and it was very outrageous. This supervisor knew that he had caught me off guard. He did this with little care for me and with complete latitude. This was an almost out of body experience for me, as I watched the cash and merchandise rapidly exchange hands. Part of me wanted to pull my pistol out on him and disburse the interacting civilians with a few airborne shots. This deal went down and was completed in a matter of minutes. I was still speechless and in shock, as he returned us back to base, through the Bien Hoa city gate. The rest of that patrol was just a blur.

This was open and blatant corruption. The crime had gone down in my presence, and it had been very disturbing. Although I had been an unwitting accomplice, I knew that if I said or did nothing about this, then I could be culpable, as well. After a few sleepless nights, I determined that this incident and others had to be reported to the appropriate authorities. So, on my day off and with considerable trepidation, I walked into the USAF Office of Special Investigations (OSI). Everything that I could recall, was reported. The agent that I talked to seemed very ill at ease, with my extraordinary revelations. All of my information was taken down and I returned back to my barracks mentally exhausted, overwhelmed and wary of what the consequences might be. It would not be long before the ramifications commenced.

A few days later, I was notified that I had to report to a high ranking, noncommissioned officer, at our squadron HQ. I was told, in essence, I had not been performing my job in an acceptable manner and that I would be removed from my high-profile day job and placed immediately on the grave shift. Completely flabbergasted, I really had no words. This script had been completely flipped on me and there was a feeling of complete emptying, betrayal and defeat.

The next graveyard shift, I reported to work with a new crew, and it was very awkward. I didn't know how this had been explained to my new coworkers, if at all. The system had failed. It was corrupted and it had needed a fall guy. I was told by my friends on day shift that the flight chief was giddy, when he announced that the "backstabbers" had now been removed. In other words, with the last personnel impediment removed, all those involved with ongoing corruption schemes now had virtual "freedom of commerce".

I don't know all of the names of those that were bad cops, but the extent of the corruption was deep and entrenched. I was already well into my short calendar and had come to the conclusion that there may no longer be a voluntary contribution of services on my part. However, I would otherwise put my time in, until I was finished there. Days later, I was at the army gate, with an army cop. It was dark and we had both been passing the time, with small talk. There had just been the regular, light traffic. I happened to notice that my fellow policeman was fixated on something, and it seemed to be a small glassy object, very close to us, on the ground. When we checked the object out, it was a glass jar, filled with something. Upon a closer look, the jar was packed with what looked like gunpowder and metal objects. We both now recognized this object was an improvised explosive device (IED). What was most destressing is who had placed this, when had it been placed and how could someone possibly get so close and not be noticed? It was truly, very alarming. After the initial shock, I radioed a request for an emergency dispatch of an explosive ordinance disposal (EOD) unit. They came almost immediately, and it was a VNAF unit. The specialist nonchalantly picked up the bomb with his hands, then opened it up and poured the contents out. The metal objects in it were several bent Vietnamese coins, which were sourced for shrapnel. The expert told us that this would have been soon, set off by natural heat, as the sun rose and ignited the gas and powder. The jar was warm to the touch and there was still a hint of ammonia gas. He went on to tell us that i.e., we were inside the kill zone. After EOD left, we kept struggling with the question of how someone had very skillfully put this simple bomb together and had come so close to completing their mission. Inevitably, I asked myself, if this was retaliation for all the damage that I had done to impede all the drugs and systematic corruption on this installation, as well as "removing" a key witness? The answer that I continuously come to is that I will always believe that it was.

Gate crash

There was another memorable close call at this gate, months earlier. I had a USAF pickup stopped and was chatting to the stationary occupants. An army duce and a half (two and a half ton) truck coming to the gate, at the same time had lost its brakes and the driver was frantically blowing the horn. Barely before the crunching impact, I dove away, just missing being crushed to death, under the heavy truck tires. The crash sideswiped the driver's side of the pickup and struck our small gate. It was virtually destroyed and the soldier in the gate was also fast enough to escape injury. The driver of the truck had gotten out, after it eventually came to a stop. He was noticeably upset and was visibly trembling. With the exception of a few scratches and bruises, I escaped major injury. As I was shaken myself, I had to be relieved for the rest of the shift. I was taken back to CSC and arrived trembling and may have even been in shock. The one good thing that came from this incident is that the small gate was replaced by a new and much nicer one.

I had had a rough history, at this particular post. There had been several confrontations, with some being very unpleasant. I had witnessed numerous enemy attacks and there was the cobra adventure. There had been a near fatal vehicle accident and now, a probable assassination attempt. The writing was on the wall, and it was time for me to leave this place, while I was still walking and breathing.

Conclusion

My time in Vietnam finally concluded in June of 1972. Metaphorically, our freedom bird left Bien Hoa, just as the sun was setting over the darkening coastline. The beauty of the South China Sea faded and bade me farewell. The dragon's lair was now behind us. I believe that we had a headwind, up to Japan, where we landed. The bright and colorful lights of Tokyo were so beautiful at night. After a timely stopover, we crossed the pond for the last time and then landed in California. Some very tired, but also very happy servicemen walked down the ramp. Finally, we were back on American soil. Here, I was certain that there would not be any rocket attacks or sinister IED placements. After being put up for the night, I was able to get mustered out of the service the next day. It was a lengthy process, and my body was running on coffee, disbelief and adrenaline. The next day, I caught a civilian flight and formerly returned to Charleston, SC. It would be some time before my body and mind got back in sync with the new time zone and environment. Decompressing would be a gradual process. My life as a civilian was now restarting and using the G.I. bill, I was determined to begin college classes, in the fall. As the days and weeks went by, my time in the war seemed to be a dream.

Part of the long process of readjustment and healing was reconnecting with family and friends. My brother and I happened to meet a first cousin, a little while after we came back. He had a privileged life and was a multisport athlete in high school. Yet somehow, he did not go into the military and serve, as we and so many others of our young generation had done. His father was well connected, and he was shielded in life, to a fault. Upon immediate recognition of us, he stated with a smirk, "You didn't have it so bad in Vietnam…You were in the Air Force"! This was a completely false and contemptable statement and caught my brother and I off guard. This was a purposely condescending; arrogant rationalization and we were both enraged and speechless.

Unfortunately for him, karma would intervene, and he would end up being the biggest failure in life that I ever had the great misfortune of knowing. His father had worked in real estate construction and associated businesses. He had groomed his son, our cousin, to eventually take over the business that he had built up over a lifetime. Unfortunately, coddled and inept, this individual was never going to be anything like his father. After handing over some of the reins, practically everything that he touched was a disaster and most of this was seen by our uncle, before his death. A very promising future had been squandered and more than one life had been adversely affected. Now deceased, this cousin's life ended abysmally.

With this being said, like so many other combat veterans, the war would always be part of me physically and psychologically. After graduating from college and working for several years, there would inevitably be escalating, psychological events. After the Veterans Administration realized that this was an overwhelming phenomenon of numerous Vietnam veterans, they have evolved to be more receptive and amenable to the needs of these veterans. There are varying levels of Post Traumatic Stress Disorder or PTSD from combat zones. I am very happy to still be here. Too many of my fellow comrades in arms don't have that luxury. They paid the ultimate price, and their names are inscribed on "The Wall" in Washington D.C. I have visited this beautiful, but somber place, to pay my respects to all and the ones that I have known. Our ever-dwindling population will always have indelible memories of this occasion. Lastly, I am very proud to have served voluntarily and wear the military uniform of "The United States of America".

My Story

Just

Through these eyes, I have seen innumerable things.

Understand

With this cognizance, I have known life at its best and worst.

Then

In this heart, I sensed emotions and am the sole survivor of this animate vessel.

And

At times, I have struggled through these experiences, yet I prevailed.

Now

With these vivid recollections, I have written my story.

Printed by Libri Plureos GmbH in Hamburg,
Germany